THE
RICHARDSONS AT
CHASTLETON

THE RICHARDSONS *AT* CHASTLETON

The story of the family who rented
Chastleton House from 1896 to 1933

Martin J Elson

THE CHOIR PRESS

First published in the United Kingdom in 2016 by
The Choir Press

ISBN 978-1-910864-34-0

www.martinelson9@gmail.com

Contents

Contents

Preface

Study of the Richardson family, who rented Chastleton for a 37-year period between 1896 and 1933, allows us to observe the rise and varied fortunes of a resourceful family over more than three centuries.

The Richardson family's ancestors have a fascinating tale to tell, whether dominating the making of quality silver in Chester in the eighteenth century, opening up lead mines and smelters in North Wales, or helping Brunel to achieve some of his most exciting rail projects during the Victorian era.

Charles Taswell Richardson, who rented Chastleton with his wife, May, survived the ravages of a tea planter's existence in Assam before going on to invest in, and run, successful tea businesses in both India and Ceylon.

There are links to the introduction of 'japanning' in Birmingham, tennis at the Wimbledon Championships in the 1880s and the participation of women in the Royal Air Force in the Great War. Stories of mini submarines in 1916, life in an Indian cavalry regiment, and courage in the trenches of Northern France help to fill in this extraordinary canvas.

Insights into daily life and below stairs organisation at Chastleton, the activities and organisation of the servants and how the family interacted with their contemporaries in and around North Oxfordshire round out this picture of life in Victorian and Edwardian England.

Preface

The 'Richardsons' referred to are subject to shorthand reference in the text. Among close family members and contemporaries are found:

CTR Charles Taswell Richardson (1853–1920) tea planter, who rented Chastleton House.

WSC Walter Seymour Carson, who married Violet Taswell Richardson in 1916, and had a career in the Royal Navy.

AGSA Augustus Gordon Stewart Alexander, an Indian Army officer, who married Rosemary Taswell Richardson in 1931.

CR Charles Richardson (1814–1896), a civil engineer who worked with Brunel and lived the major part of his life in Bristol.

IWJ Irene Whitmore Jones (1870–1955), owner of Chastleton House during the Richardsons' tenancy.

EC Edward Carson, father of WSC; famous Irish unionist politician, barrister and judge.

Seven persons with the name Richard Richardson have been identified during the study! Each has been numbered for ease of reference in the text, and is referred to in capitals in the genealogy below. Richard 1 (1674–1729), for example, was a goldsmith in Chester, and Richard 7 (1894–1915) was a lieutenant in the Royal Warwickshire Regiment during the Great War.

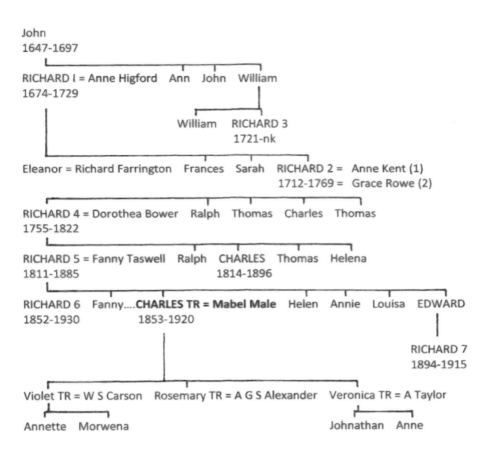

1 *Genealogy of the Richardson family.*

Acknowledgements

For access to information, including photographs, I am particularly indebted to the following: Dawn McDonald, Visitor Services Manager, and Seb Conway, Steward at the National Trust's Chastleton House. Lawrie Thompson went out of his way to provide much information from his past researches at Chastleton. Sue McDougall, Angela Joule and other volunteers at Chastleton House also assisted with new material.

Peter Smith gave me a personal tour of Portmeadow Aerodrome. Dave Nobbs of the Chipping Norton History Society found details of the location of the drowning of Charles Taswell Richardson, and Robin Darvill-Smith, Archivist at University College, Oxford, furnished an excellent photograph of Richard Richardson (RR6), a student at Oxford in 1872.

Peter Wright provided information on the RAF during the Great War, and the staff of the Royal Regiment of Fusiliers (Royal Warwickshire) Museum in Warwick found details of the service career of Richard Francis Richardson (RR7). Trevor Thompson of the Clifton and Hotwells Improvement Society (Bristol) proved an enthusiastic advocate of Charles Richardson, the engineer of the Severn Tunnel. The University of Gloucestershire library allowed access to information on the Richardson Journal. The staff of the Oxford Local History Centre responded positively to my requests for various photographic and other documents. John Pratt made useful, and always amusing, comments on the draft text.

I would like to thank Meg Humphries of Green Star Proof Reading for work on the text, and Miles Bailey, Rachel Woodman and Adrian Sysum for production assistance and their guidance.

Illustration acknowledgements

The National Trust: 5, 7, 22, 35, 36, 38, 39, 40, 41, 42, 43, 44 front and rear cover picture, and diagrams in Annex 1. Ridgway, M. *Chester Silver 1727–1837* and the author: 1. Oxfordshire History Centre: 2, 3, 4, 8, 33, 34. English Heritage: 6. Country Life: 9. Local Government Gazette: 12. Walker T., *The Severn Tunnel*: 14. University College, Oxford: 15. Angela Joule, 16, 17, 18. Marlborough College: 20. Royal Warwickshire Regiment Museum: 21. Lewis, G., *Carson: The Man Who Divided Ireland*: 22. National Archives, Kew: 25. Wright, P. *The RFC in Oxfordshire*: 26 (first edition), 27 & 28 (second edition). The RAF Museum, Hendon: 29. Royal Geographical Society: 32. Gordon, C., *Cotswold Arts and Crafts Architecture*: 45.

CHAPTER 1

The early Richardson years

An uneventful history?

Hidden away among the lanes of North Oxfordshire can be found one of the most enchanting and unaltered Jacobean country houses in England. Chastleton House was built in 1612 for Walter Jones, a lawyer (part of a family of wealthy wool merchants), originally from South Wales. It is a fine example of the work of local masons using the dark honey-coloured Hornton stone typical of this part of the Cotswolds.[1]

Jones had acquired the land on which the house stands from Robert Catesby, one of the Gunpowder Plotters. Demolishing the Catesby residence, he built a tall, compact, four-storey manor house arranged around a central courtyard.

Visitors to the property will see the impressive symmetrical south-facing frontage of the building and the two prominent staircase towers projecting from its eastern and western walls (Figure 2). A notable feature of the top floor of the house is the Long Gallery. This 72-foot-long space has the longest barrel-vaulted ceiling of its type in the country.

Around the house are four acres of gardens. These include the Best Garden, with 24 pieces of topiary arranged in a circle, a number of strategically planted ancient oak trees to lead the visitor's eye into the surrounding fields, and an extensive Kitchen Garden. Two croquet lawns are found on the North Terrace, reflecting the reputation of Chastleton as the place where the rules of croquet were first codified by Walter Whitmore-Jones in 1865 (Figure 3). To the west of the house there was, prior to the

2 *The south facade of Chastleton House during the Richardsons' tenure. The topiary cockeral looking over from Chastleton churchyard was a prominent feature.*

Richardson's time, a kitchen garden. By 1910 there were new hedges and a greenhouse (Figure 4).

The property includes a stable yard, with accompanying Brewhouse and servants' accommodation. The 'below stairs' areas are largely above ground because of the high level of the rock platform on which the house is built. Arranged around the Dairy Court are a basement kitchen, the Servants Hall, larders, a dairy and a large cellar running the length of the house. A fuller account of the basement layout is given in Annex 2.

Chastleton remained in the ownership of members of the Jones family for nearly four hundred years. In 1991, the property was acquired from Mrs Clutton-Brock (a descendent of Walter Jones) by the National Heritage Memorial Fund, and transferred to the National Trust. Following extensive repairs and conservation work, the property was opened to the public in 1997.

The Jones family ran an estate of over 1,200 acres initially, with the rents from a number of tenanted farms being their major intended source of income. Early optimism resulted from trading in wool, the country's most valuable commodity at the time.

3 *The North Terrace at Chastleton, with the croquet lawn and tennis court in the foreground. A thatched rustic-style pavilion can also be seen.*

Problems arose from the support by the family for the royalist cause in the Civil War. Defeat for the Royalists led to the loss of most of the family money, with the payment of financial reparations to the parliamentarians. The decline of the wool trade, as competition from other clothing materials grew, also did not help.

The Chastleton Diaries shows the day-to-day activities of the Jones family during the eighteenth century. Tasks such as presiding at the local assizes, acting as guardians of the local workhouse in Chipping Norton, or raising a local militia to protect against agricultural riots at the time of the repeal of the Corn Laws in the 1830s, occupied much of the energies of the head of the family.[2]

There were also problems seeking to remain solvent as agricultural fortunes declined. Tenants on the Chastleton estate would regularly fail to pay all or part of their rents, and with few alternative sources of income, attempts were made to cut costs. In 1840, John Henry Whitmore-Jones sought to rent out the house, but without success. To save money, the family moved to Warren House in Dawlish, only returning to Chastleton in 1846.

In late Victorian times, matters did not improve. Life for successive owners of Chastleton consisted of balancing a number of mortgages on parts of the estate and using local connections to seek new ones. Attempts were made to sell off individual farms without success, as the land, especially on the adjacent Chastleton Hill, was not of particularly high fertility.

John Henry's third son, Walter Whitmore-Jones, secured a job in the civil service through the influence of Disraeli, a family acquaintance, but soon left as he could not stand the routine and methods of working at the time. He went on to publish new rules for croquet in 1865, and is credited with producing an early version of the definitive version of golf croquet played today. Along with a brother and sister, he also invented various parlour games, such as *Squails* and the *Chinese Imperial Game of Frogs and Toads*, which were marketed through Jaques, the croquet club manufacturers. Unsurprisingly, none of these ventures led to any great riches for the family.[3]

By the end of the 1860s, the property was owned by widower

4 *The West Garden at Chastleton House.*

Mary Whitmore-Jones. Although she lived until 1915, she handed over the house to her nephew Thomas Whitmore-Harris. One condition was that he changed his name to Whitmore-Jones, which he did later. However, by the 1890s, the house had become too much of a burden, and it was advertised for rent.

Affluent tenants

The family who secured the tenancy was Mr and Mrs Charles Taswell Richardson (CTR), who rented the house over a 37-year period until 1933. The agreed rent was £350 per annum, approximately £40,000 a year at today's prices. Figure 5 shows the family sitting on the front steps of the house, including the three daughters Violet, Rosemary and Veronica, in 1913, just before the start of the Great War.

5 *The Richardson family in 1913. Left to right: Violet, May, Veronica, Charles and Rosemary.*

6 *Capenhurst Hall near Chester, where Charles Taswell Richardson lived as a child.*

Charles Taswell Richardson was born in December 1853, within one of the foremost families in Cheshire.[4] He was one of seven children, made up of four daughters and three sons, of the Reverend Richard Richardson of Capenhurst Hall, near Chester.[5] During his youth, CTR therefore lived in a substantial rectory in Cheshire, which had been built with wealth inherited from the family's silversmithing and lead mining activities. Capenhurst Hall in the 1880s is shown in Figure 6.[6] The 'Taswell Richardson' name originated from the marriage of Charles' father to Fanny Taswell in 1830.

At the time the Chastleton lease was secured, Charles was married to Mabel 'May' Rose Male.[7] Violet, their first child, had been born in 1894, Rosemary, the second, in 1899 and Veronica the third, some 13 years later in 1912 (see Figure 1). When she arrived at Chastleton, May was only 24, and already had a young child of two, whereas her husband was 19 years older, being 43 years of age.[8]

Charles Taswell Richardson is listed in the 1911 census as of 'independent means'. He had been a tea planter in India in the 1870s, and had also inherited wealth from the family's silver business in Chester. CTR was an active sociable man; soon after moving to Chastleton he became a well connected figure in the North Oxfordshire area. He was a member of the Heythrop Hunt, and of the Cheltenham Racecourse.

In addition, he served on the Chipping Norton Board of Guardians, the body that managed the Chipping Norton workhouse. Here he would have been involved in re-building the workhouse after a serious fire in 1911. He was Secretary of the Chastleton Hill Golf Club, which operated from 1895 to 1920, and was a keen churchgoer, often reading the lesson at services at Chastleton Church.

The eldest Richardson daughter, Violet, married Walter Seymour Carson RN at the height of the Great War in 1916 and had two children. Walter was the younger son of Sir Edward Carson's first marriage. Edward Carson was a leading Unionist politician, a member of Asquith's Cabinet in 1916 and a barrister and judge. He led resistance to Irish Home Rule, and was credited with being the chief architect and creator of Northern Ireland. However, he still had time to sign the banns for, and attend, the Chastleton wedding!

The second daughter, Rosemary, remained at Chastleton throughout her 20s, only marrying Augustus Alexander in 1931, when she was 31 years old. He was a captain, and later a colonel, in the Central India Horse. He excelled at polo, but also liked hunting and shooting.

The youngest daughter, Veronica, was born just before the Great War, in 1912. She married Arthur Taylor at the age of 19. Taylor was descended from a prominent family of Birmingham manufacturers, bankers and landowners. They had two children: Jonathan, who was born in 1934, and Anne, who was born in 1940.

After leaving Chastleton early in 1933, unwilling to pay a proposed increase in rent, May Richardson lived at *Hillside*, an impressive Victorian property set back from the Chipping Norton to Moreton-in-Marsh road. She died in December 1933 and is buried in Chastleton churchyard. Her cause of death was given as pneumonia. Violet Richardson, the first daughter, died in 1968, aged 74, and is also buried at Chastleton. Rosemary lived to the age of 95, before her death in Banbury in 1984. Veronica died in 1966, aged 54.

The early years at Chastleton

It is not known why the Richardsons chose Chastleton as their home, and the family appears to have had no previous connections to Oxfordshire. The Richardsons may have seen Chastleton as a pleasant place to live and to bring up their young children. It was also, conveniently, within a short distance of Leamington Spa, where May's mother, Marion Male, still lived.

From taped interviews, held by the National Trust, we know most about Rosemary's daily life. As a young girl she would spend her time in the nursery with her governess, sometimes with her cousins, including her cousin Katherine from Birmingham. During the day she would also ride or walk her donkey or pony around the garden and play outdoors. There appear to have been no piano lessons. Rosemary firmly states in one interview, taped by the National Trust, 'I was not musical'.

Dogs were a favourite of the Richardson daughters: they are shown on wedding photographs posed on the front steps of the house, and there are two shown on the photo of Violet and Rosemary sitting on a car outside the front door (see Figure 7). The only marked dogs' grave at Chastleton is located in a border on the eastern side of the North Terrace. The stone records *Babette* (1900), *Julie* (1908) and *Nankie* (1910).

Chastleton House has over 30 rooms spread over its four

7 *Rosemary and Violet Richardson outside the front door of Chastleton House.*

floors. The Richardsons appear to have regularly used only around ten of them, in the lower part of the house. The Great Hall and Oak Parlour on the ground floor were utilised, but May preferred the White Parlour, also on the ground floor, for day-to-day activities. The Great Parlour functioned as the dining room, and Charles and May used what is now the Sheldon Room, on the first floor, as their bedroom.[9] The room layout of the house is shown in Annex 1.

During some of her childhood years, Rosemary had a bedroom next to the domestic staff at the top of the house. This type of arrangement was not unknown in other country houses, as young members of the family often identified with servants nearer their own age. This phenomenon is noted by Horn in her book *The Rise and Fall of the Victorian Servant.*[10]

When the Richardsons moved in, part of the ceiling of the Long Gallery was missing due to water leakage through the roof that had gone on for many years, as a *Country Life* picture of 1902 shows (Figure 8). This was re-instated by Irene Whitmore Jones

8 *Damage to the Long Gallery ceiling can be seen on the left of this picture, taken for* Country Life *in 1902.*

(IWJ) in 1904. Part of the panelling in the Long Gallery was also removed by IWJ as a memento of her time at Chastleton, and installed in the Dower House, next door in Chastleton village, where she moved in 1897. It remains there today.

The Richardsons were keen to see improvements to the level of maintenance of the property. Attempts were made to secure repairs to the damaged gates giving access to the stable yard. As the Whitmore-Joneses seemed reluctant to make the repairs, over several letters now held by the Oxford Records Centre, May Richardson wrote to Irene Whitmore Jones offering to pay for the work. In one such letter she says: 'Charlie [CTR] is away, but they are such an awful nuisance to us that that we would be willing to pay the cost of £5.10s on his return if we can have them done at once'. May even recommended a local resident, Skelcher, to do the work, 'as he seems short of a job at the moment'. Earlier there had been problems with the water supply, CTR writing to IWJ that the supply was 'in a bad way . . . pipes are blocked above the tank and it is overflowing the road . . . the nails around the water reservoir are rotten and the water supply may be contaminated'. There were also problems with the cottage rented for the coachmen in the village, with water entering through the front door.

Messrs George H Gray of Moreton-in-Marsh appears to have been the jobbing builder for repairs at Chastleton at this time. In 1909, the Richardsons used Gray to carry out repairs in the stables at a cost of £63. Part of the roof of the stables was replaced, and a new window frame and door was installed in the room above the harness room. In 1910 a number of window panes were also renewed (Figure 9).[11]

There was no electricity in the Long Gallery on the top floor of the house during the Richardsons' time. The servants needed to walk this way to get to their bedrooms. Candles and, later, torches were used to assist this process, which was regarded by some of them as a 'spooky' experience. The presence of a number of bats, flitting among the rafters at the top of the house, may have contributed to this feeling.

At the age of 14, Rosemary went to boarding school in Bexhill-on-Sea with her cousin Katherine, from Birmingham. By the age of 17, towards the end of the Great War, she was learning to drive. This freed her to visit friends in the North Oxfordshire area more easily, and go on horse rides and hunts with them. She also played squash, as two of her friends lived in houses that had squash courts attached. The family acquired early motor cars, two of which are shown in various photographs (see Figures 7, 40 and 42). The children might occasionally play badminton in the Long Gallery if the weather was inclement. Shuttlecocks were found below the floorboards by the National Trust during restoration of the house in the 1990s.

The family had annual holidays away from Chastleton, normally

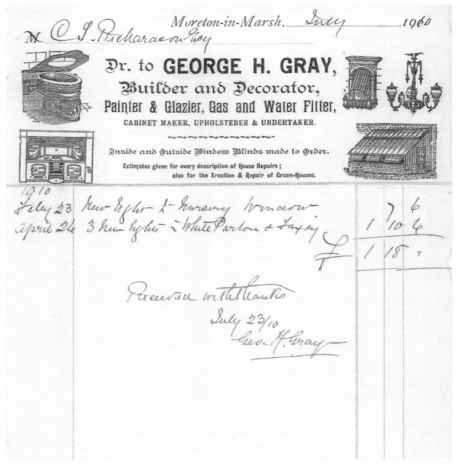

Moreton-in-Marsh. *July* *1960*

Dr. to **GEORGE H. GRAY,**
Builder and Decorator,
Painter & Glazier, Gas and Water Fitter,
CABINET MAKER, UPHOLSTERER & UNDERTAKER.

Inside and Outside Window Blinds made to Order.

Estimates given for every description of House Repairs;
also for the Erection & Repair of Green-Houses.

9 *Bill from Messrs Gray, builders, for replacing window panes at Chastleton House.*

lasting two weeks, often going to the seaside in the south-west of England, or even to France. On one trip to France, Rosemary was ill and stayed longer than planned. At such times, there would be extra work for those remaining at the house: the servants would carry out a full spring clean, including taking up and beating the carpets and scrubbing the floors. The Head Gardener acted as caretaker while the family were away.

Violet Richardson left the house in 1916 upon her marriage,

leaving Rosemary and her much younger sister Veronica as the resident children. When Violet and her husband later went to India with the Royal Navy, their children and the nanny stayed at Chastleton, where they were taught along with the Richardson children.

The Richardsons employed more servants than the Whitmore-Joneses. Notably, three full-time gardeners were employed, a larger outside staff than at any other time in the history of the house. As a result, much work was done to improve the garden. There were also two grooms for the horses.

The 1911 census return for Chastleton House lists eight servants in residence. In addition, the garden staff lived in a cottage in the village, rented from Irene Whitmore Jones for £6 per year. Additional part-time staff were also employed. Those listed in the April 1911 census are:

- Lillian Truman, 40, governess, single;
- Eva Glane, 35, cook, single;
- Mabel Rose, 22, lady's maid, single;
- Fannie Bishop, 25, housemaid, single;
- Mary Bates, 23, housemaid, single;
- Lizzie Holyfield, 17, kitchen maid, single;
- Herbert Matmant, 33, butler, single; and
- Arthur Billingham, 17, footman, single.[12]

Lillian Truman was a Norland Nurse, a graduate of the most prestigious nursery training institution in the UK. The Norland School was the first college in the country to offer proper childcare training. Based originally in London, the courses were taught along Froebel's educational principles (the Kindergarten Movement). Early publicity for the school stated it was 'the training school for ladies as children's nurses'.[13] Students wore uniforms at college and also in the workplace after they had secured positions with families.

The children's nurse did not eat with the servants and, as Leth-bridge states, 'Norland nurses did not clean, wipe, launder or sweep; their concern was solely the tending of their charges' moral and psychological development'.[14] Many commentators consider that governesses were in an isolated position, caught between servants and their masters. However, there was no evidence of this at Chastleton.

Cheshire silversmiths and lead miners

The Richardson family history can be traced back to Knightwick, in the Malvern Hills, where John Richardson was born in 1647. At the age of 14, he went to London as a goldsmith's apprentice. He later had eight children, two of whom were to become goldsmiths in Chester, Richard I and his younger brother William. The genealogy for the family is given in Figure 1.

Richard Richardson I (RR1), his third child, having completed an apprenticeship with his father, moved to Chester just before the city's gold and silver assay office opened in 1701.[15] Admitted as a freeman in 1703, he set up a shop and manufacturing workshop for gold and silver items in Eastgate Row in the centre of the city. Much of the silver made, such as communion cups and candle-sticks, was for churches in the region.

Richard Richardson I also had wide interests in the lead industry in North Wales.[16] The mines were situated in an area of carboniferous limestone running north west–south east from Flint to south of Mold. The mineral was found in veins in the limestone and was difficult to extract. Richardson was a partner in the Maeshafn Mine near Mold in the 1720s. The family also leased land for a lead smelter at Llanerch-Y-Mor on the Flintshire coast. RR1 was the Assay Master at the Chester Assay Office from 1713 until his early death in 1729.

Much of the mineral-rich land in North Wales, including land where gold, copper, coal and lead was found, was owned by the

Grosvenor Estate.[17] They had acquired this during the 1630s, when Charles I, desperate to augment his finances, had been selling land. The Grosvenors then leased out the mineral rights, most commonly on 21-year leases, and the Richardson family were one of the prominent Chester merchant families who were successful bidders. Other land was owned by the city companies of Chester, and they also leased it in similar fashion. The links between lead mining and silversmithing were clear, silver being a by-product of the mining process. It is estimated that on average between six and 18 ounces of silver per ton of lead were achieved from mines in the area at this time.

Richard Richardson II (RR2) was born in 1712 and was the seventh child of RR1, and was the most prolific Chester silver-maker of his era. Apprenticed to his father, he was admitted as a freeman of the city in 1732, and subsequently became an alderman in 1754 and mayor in 1757. Apart from these civic duties, he was also Assay Master in Chester from 1761 until he died in 1769.

RR2 had widespread interests in mining: Ridgway notes that 'he entered into a covenant regarding 20 mines in North Wales, only weeks before he died'.[18] He had earlier taken over land at Llanferres from RR1, and in the early 1740s he purchased mineral rights at Minera near Mold. In 1741 he took out a lease of 40 years' duration on land at Pentrobin; a conical lead smelter was duly erected on the site in 1751, and was originally fuelled by charcoal.

Richardson further enhanced the security of supply of his mine outputs by purchasing a share in a ship called the *Chester Trader*; this also speeded up the delivery of lead ores from the Dee Estuary. Up to 20 traders would buy shares in such ships at this time to help spread their risks. Many were still wary of sole investments after the 'South Sea Bubble' of 1720. The lead was exported to Liverpool and London, and some then saw its way to the continent (see Figure 10).

The Richardsons, father and son, were eminent in their trade. They are regarded as the most important goldsmith in Chester in the 18th century. The Grosvenor Museum, which has three display cases of Richardson silver, states that 'the greatest Chester silversmith was Richard Richardson 2'. He specialised in the Rococo style, which was particularly popular between 1740 and 1770. Canon Ridgway's definitive study *Chester Silver 1727–1837* devotes 35 pages to RR2's output of silver, far more than to any other Chester silversmith.[19]

Following the death of RR2 in 1769, his son and natural successor, Richard Richardson (RR4), was only 14 years of age. In order to protect the family legacy and activities of the business, RR3, the son of William Richardson, supervised the silver workshop, and other aspects of the business until RR4 had completed his apprenticeship and had been made a freeman. RR3 was not a silversmith, but worked as a chandler and, later, in finance in London. From 1785 to 1791, RR4 was nevertheless the Assay Master at the Chester office.

RR2 had eight children by his first wife, Anne Kent. When she died in 1766, he married Grace Rowe. RR2's death left a number of young children to be cared for, and they were informally 'adopted', with Grace Rowe's consent, by his elder sister Eleanor and her husband Richard Farrington (see Figure 1). They secured an apprenticeship for RR4, and training for another brother, Ralph Richardson, so that the family's mining interests could be adequately looked after. Ralph managed the lead smelters in the possession of the family, and also purchased coal mining rights in Wales at this time.

Richard Farrington had a range of mining interests in Scotland as well as North Wales, some shared with RR2.[20] Upon the death of Farrington in 1772, RR4 inherited his mining interests. On Eleanor's death two years later, he received a further 25 per cent of the value of the mines in her will, helping make him a wealthy man.

By 1791, the Richardsons had disposed of their premises in Chester to jewellers Butt and Guy; Butt and Guy were most recently taken over by Mappin and Webb in 1968. RR4 went on to acquire the manor of Capenhurst, comprising just over 50 acres of land four miles north of Chester, from Lord Cholmondeley. First a farm was built, and then Capenhurst Hall, two years later. The hall was a substantial country home, with stables and room for a number of servants. RR4 appears to have finally severed his connections with Chester silver working in 1796.

RR4 married Dorothea Bowers in 1810 and had five children. His eldest son, the Reverend Richard Richardson (RR5) then inherited the Capenhurst estate. RR5 had matriculated at

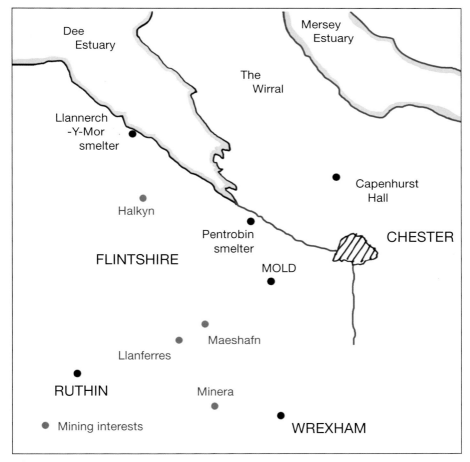

10 *Richardson mining interests in North East Wales.*

Brasenose College, Oxford in 1834 and had studied law at the Inner Temple. However, he changed his career direction, becoming an ordained priest in 1845. Capenhurst Church was subsequently built late in the 1850s. He clearly had plenty of funds for this large-scale undertaking.[21]

Charles Taswell Richardson and tea planting

Given the above background, it is not surprising that Charles Taswell Richardson, the tenant at Chastleton and the son of RR5, is listed in the 1911 Census as of independent means. He had previously resided in London before coming to the Midlands area and Chastleton. CTR had left England to work as a tea planter in Assam, India earlier in life, most likely during the late 1870s, but returned to the UK on the death of his father in 1885.

The work for a tea planter was arduous and challenging. As a manager, CTR would be supervising the clearance of native vegetation to create tea gardens, securing site boundaries and planting tea bushes.[22] Labour was usually short and needed to be recruited from other areas of India. The control of workers was not without its problems, with various strikes and protests occurring. Disease was rife, and the processing and export of the tea was also a less-than-routine process by river to Calcutta or Chittagong. Local climatic conditions affected yields, so that production was not always assured. The climate was hot and steamy, and there was a wide range of local diseases, which non-natives were particularly susceptible to.

At some point between arriving in India and 1895, CTR became a director of the Mookhamcherra Tea Company located in Sylhet, Assam, a town which has been, since 1971, in the north-eastern corner of Bangladesh.[23] Sylhet is some 250 miles inland from Calcutta, and was accessible along the Brahmaputra and Meghna rivers, along which local steamers could only ply their trade during the rainy season (Figure 11).

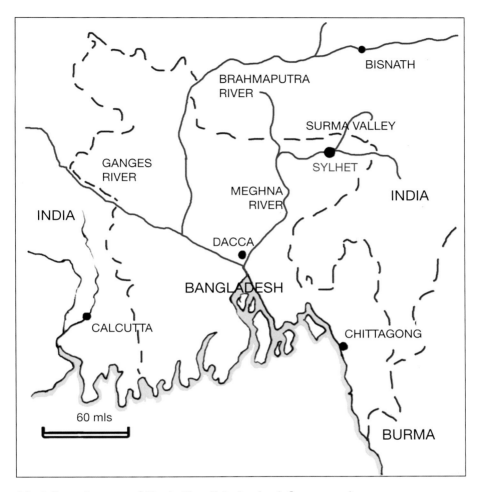

11 *Sylhet – Location of Charles Taswell Richardson's first tea garden.*

By 1895, two years before he came to Chastleton, CTR had merged his interests with others to form the East India and Ceylon Tea Company (EICTC), where he is listed as a director. His address at this point is given as 31 Binswood Ave, Leamington Spa in Warwickshire. This is a substantial Victorian property in the historic part of the town, built in the early 1830s, and currently a private school.

The prospectus seeking capital for the new company was published in the *St James Gazette* in October 1895. The aim was to take over and amalgamate the following as going concerns:

- The Doolabcherra Tea Company (Sylhet, Assam);
- The Mookhamcherra Tea Company (Sylhet, Assam);
- The Mahaousa Tea Company (Ceylon);
- The Blackwater Estate (Ceylon); and
- The Hapugastenne and Walawadowa Estates, both in Ceylon.

The merger of these holdings would give plantations totalling 12,660 acres, of which only 3,630 acres (30 per cent) was already in production. Of the planted land, 2,500 acres were in India and 1,130 acres in Ceylon. This would give considerable scope for future extension of the planted area without acquiring new land.[24]

The prospectus states that although tea plantations were generally very profitable, they had yet to attract interest from non-specialist UK investors. With China no longer the main source of supply and India and Ceylon producing 80 per cent of world tea production, the attractiveness of such assets was rapidly growing. By having estates in Ceylon and India, the new consolidated company would combine the advantages peculiar to each and consequently achieve the best average result. There was claimed to be an adequate supply of machinery, plentiful labour and good local management to maximise the value of the assets. The estates in the offer were lucrative, with the profits given as £9,874 in 1892 and £12,586 in 1895. A six per cent annual dividend was predicted for investors, based on previous results.[25]

CTR was very well connected to some of the main 'actors' in the Indian tea trade. The Chairman of his new EICTC was P R Buchanan. Buchanan was an expert in tea planting methods, and the management of tea estates who had advised, among others, John Muir, a prominent Scottish planter, who created two major consolidations, the North and South Sylhet tea companies, in 1882.

Buchanan had set up a London tea brokers in 1871. He soon acquired warehouses in the Thames Estuary (some of Richardson's tea would most likely have ended up in these). Buchanan formed a partnership with the Finlay Group in 1894. The Agents in Calcutta for the EICTC were Finlay Muir and Co., and the Secretaries and Managing Agents were P R Buchanan and Co., with head offices in Leadenhall Street, London.

Richardson even went as far as promoting some of Buchanan's products, one of which was the *Cookes Patent Tea Sorter.* This remarkable device graded tea leaves, which were fed into a hopper at the top of the machine. This work was previously done by hand-sieving, with baskets made from bamboo.

Reflecting the tight-knit nature of the tea trade, the London sale agent for the Tea Sorter was P R Buchanan, and its Calcutta agents were Finlay Muir! Charles Taswell Richardson provided a testimonial for the machine, which was installed at Mookham-cherra, and this is printed on a contemporary advertisement (see Figure 12). He states: 'I consider it the best sorter I have ever seen at work'.[26]

The other Director of EICTC, Stratton Bulnois, was a tea broker in London, trading under the name of Bulnois, Drew and Company. Bulnois was a Conservative MP and a friend of Conan Doyle. Proof of this is his listing in the visitors' book at the Conan Doyle home at Undershaw, near Hindhead, in Surrey.

The East India Company

The tea industry in India originated in the state of Assam, in the north-eastern corner of India. The first tea plants growing wild were discovered there in 1821. Tea plantations were opened from 1835 onwards, after the East India Company had set up a Tea Committee to promote the trade in 1834.

12 *The tea sorting machine endorsed by Charles Taswell Richardson.*

Tea plantations developed in India in an attempt to break the Chinese monopoly of cultivation, which had resulted in very high prices in the UK. The British Government accorded high priority to the process, with the East India Company offering land (often rent free) to any Europeans who agreed to cultivate tea for export. Clandestine journeys, supported by the company, were undertaken to China to secure tea plant stock. Plantations were generally opened up by a speculative 'planter', who would then turn later to a managing agency house for working and additional fixed capital.[27]

Richardson went to India in the late 1870s, initially to manage tea estates, by which time the East India Company had been closed, and the trade was more directly under the control of the British Government. The Richardson Company prospectus in 1895 was an attempt to obtain more capital for his growing venture, and to increase profitability by the amalgamation of a number of smaller enterprises. This process of consolidation was typical of the period.

CTR was clearly a shrewd businessman: he had avoided the excesses of the tea 'gold rush' decade of the 1860s, where lax land acquisition rules had been brought in by the Assam Government. For example, the need for planters to deposit monies sufficient to prove they could successfully cultivate tea on their sites had been removed, and land speculation replaced tea planting as a key way of making money.

Richardson was well connected with persons, such as Buchanan and the Finlay family, who could give him sound advice in husbandry methods. He was investing at a time when the rupee was depreciating against sterling, giving owners a large one-off boost, nearly doubling their revenues. The capital investments resulting from flotation also helped to lower production and processing costs, a sure way of increasing profits.

Connections with the Bryans family

In India, CTR had joined Herbert Bryans, the son of the Reverend Francis Bryans, Vicar of Backford in Cheshire, who had gone to work on the tea plantations in 1877. The Bryans were family friends of the Richardsons.[28] Herbert Bryans was a director of the Chargola Tea Association, formed in 1891 in Sylhet. His brother Arthur Bryans was also a director. Herbert became a director of the EICTC, along with CTR.

Returning from India, Herbert Bryans was proceeding through France from Marseilles by train when he came across an area of vineyards. On an impulse he got off the train, throwing his baggage out of the windows, and spent two years in France working in, and managing, vineyards! Following his return to Britain, Herbert married Louisa Richardson, one of CTR's younger sisters.

Bryans' second career was in making stained glass windows. He was apprenticed to Charles Kempe, a world-renowned designer of such windows, whose work is found in many English cathedrals. Bryans set up his own firm in 1897, and subsequently undertook over three hundred commissions across the country, operating from workshops in Mornington Crescent in London. One commission was the design and installation of a window in Swardesten Church near Norwich to commemorate Edith Cavell, the nurse who had saved many escaping allied prisoners in Belgium.[29]

Two memorial windows were commissioned, by May Richardson, from Bryans. These were installed as the east (chancel) and west windows in Chastleton Church. The east chancel window is dedicated to May's mother, Marion Rosa Male, and carries the Bryans' characteristic 'greyhound' trade mark on the label; the second commemorates the death of Charles Taswell Richardson (Figure 13).[30]

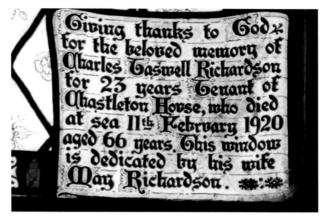

13 *Dedications on the memorial windows, designed by Herbert Bryans, in Chastleton Church.*

Charles Richardson and Brunel

Charles Taswell Richardson's great uncle, Charles Richardson (1814–1896) (CR), was a distinguished civil engineer. Educated partly in France and at the University of Edinburgh, he showed early abilities in mechanics and engineering. Securing a pupillage with Isambard Kingdom Brunel at the age of 20, he worked on schemes for the Box Tunnel near Bath, and the Thames Tunnel in

London. His journal, which covers some of the period in which he worked for Brunel, was discovered in an antique shop in 1998 and has been transcribed by Griffin (Figure 14).

Brunel was regarded as one of the most versatile and audacious engineers of the nineteenth century. One of his foremost achievements was the construction of a network of tunnels, bridges and viaducts for the Great Western Railway.[31]

Brunel heaped a lot of responsibilities on his pupils, in effect treating them as on-site engineers for the many contracts he was running concurrently. Griffin notes:

> . . . the strains and pressures borne by assistant and resident engineers find a number of illustrations in Richardson's Journal. He has to confront angry farmers, resist bribes from aspiring contractors, borrow a significant sum of money from the landlady of the inn where he is staying to meet pay requirements for his men, and to deal with a spontaneous strike over pay. There was always the possibility that Brunel himself would turn up at four o'clock in the morning and expect a report.[32]

Richardson clearly was not daunted by these responsibilities.

Subsequently Richardson became the resident engineer of the Bristol and South West Railway. He was also the instigator and first engineer of the Severn Tunnel. Later in his career, CR was in charge of designing and building improved railway connections in the centre of Bristol, around the docks, and he also managed the dualling of the line through the Severn Tunnel.

Working on the Patchway Tunnel just north of Bristol, Richardson noted the high quality of the clay that was being extracted. He subsequently bought some fields near the Tunnel and, in 1865, set up a brick-making company in Almondsbury. The Cattysbrook Brickworks produced distinctive red bricks, which line the Severn Tunnel and were used in the building of Fry's factory at Keynsham,

14 *Charles Richardson – Civil Engineer.*

as well as the offices of the Imperial Tobacco Company in Bristol. Richardson's distinctive Cattysbrook red bricks were also used in important buildings in the central part of the city. Those that survived later war-time bombing include the Granary and the Old Fishmarket. The Granary, built for Wait and James in 1869, is acknowledged as the best-preserved example of the Bristol Byzantine architectural style in the city.

Charles Richardson had a range of enthusiasms and pastimes, including walking, swimming, sketching and rowing. He was also a cricket enthusiast, inventing a spliced-handled cricket bat, and an early bowling machine. Records show he was in trouble with Brunel for organising cricket games among the Severn Tunnel workers!

His achievements were celebrated in 2014, the two-hundredth anniversary of his birth, by the erection of a blue plaque on Engineers Row, near the old docks in Bristol, by the Retired Professional Engineers Club. The Clifton and Hotwells Improvement Society also erected a plaque in Berkeley Square in Clifton in 2015, where CR lived for the last 20 years of his life.

Richard Taswell Richardson and the Wimbledon Championships

Richard Taswell Richardson (RR6) (1852–1930) was CTR's older brother. He excelled at sport, particularly cricket and tennis (see Figure 15). He was in the Marlborough College first XI from 1870–1, and in their matches against Harrow scored 118 runs and took 16 wickets. Playing at Lords, he distinguished himself by scoring 85 and 73 runs in a match against the Marylebone Cricket Club. At this time he was regarded as a batsman of 'vigorous methods'. His highest innings was 129 not out against the Royal Agricultural College at Cirencester. He played five times for the MCC. His short obituary in the *Wisden Cricketers' Almanack* for 1930 suggests he was 'a good average batsman, and in the field generally took long stop'.[33]

From Marlborough, RR6 went on to Oxford University, where he obtained a good quality Classics degree. He chose the law as a profession, was called to the Bar in 1779, and practised on the Northern Circuit.

RR6 was a nationally important singles and doubles tennis player in his early thirties. He may well have won the singles title at Wimbledon if he had not been a contemporary of the Renshaw twins and Herbert Lawford, the best players of the day.

Richardson reached the Wimbledon men's singles final on two occasions. William Renshaw defeated him in in the 1881 final in three sets, and his brother Ernest Renshaw in the 1882 final, in four sets.[34] Wimbledon tennis players in these early years were predominantly drawn from the English public schools, or from Oxbridge. Richardson, as a young barrister, won a number of regional tournaments around this time in Ireland and the North of England.

15 *Richard Taswell Richardson and the University College, Oxford cricket team in 1872. Richardson is standing on the right in the back row.*

Richard, known by Rosemary and the other Richardson children as 'Uncle Dickie', visited Chastleton many times, where he also hunted with the Heythrop. We can only imagine how good a tennis lesson he must have given his young cousins on the grass tennis court on the North Terrace at Chastleton!

CHAPTER 2

The Great War 1914–1918

Changes at Chastleton

In terms of the daily routine at Chastleton, things went on very much as before the Great War. CTR was above the age for conscription and there were no male children to go off to the trenches. The arrival of rationing in 1917 had little effect, as the house was largely self-sufficient for garden produce, and the family had a couple of cows for daily milking. Greenhouses allowed a wide range of produce to be grown. Rosemary volunteered for the Royal Air Force early in 1918, and this is described below.

The Richardsons were heavily involved in parish welfare. They were the largest subscribers to the Chastleton Coal Club. This locally-organised scheme encouraged thrift, with sixteen Chastleton families putting aside one shilling a month, over a year, to help buy coal in bulk. Honorary subscriptions to top up the fund were made by more wealthy benefactors in the parish. As a result each family received 15cwt of coal for a subscription of 12 shillings.

In 1916 subscribers included; the vicar of Chastleton (Rev G A Sneyd) who contributed one guinea, the Whitmore-Jones family, who added two guineas, and the Richardsons, a further four guineas. This, together with purchase at wholesale prices, allowed a greater amount of coal to be delivered to the railhead at Chipping Norton. The coal was then transported to Chastleton free of charge by local farmers, and distributed just prior to Christmas. A Chastleton Clothing Club was operated along the same lines at this time, with tokens being given out for the purchase of clothes.

16 *KitebrookVoluntary Aided Hospital, showing the open windows of the first floor hospital ward.*

As some of the male servants went to war, women took over their jobs. Jessie Rolf (1893–1985), born in Scotland, came to Moreton-in-Marsh in 1916, and was employed by May Richardson as a chauffeuse. She also carried out ambulance driving and delivery duties at the Voluntary Aid Detachment (VAD) auxiliary hospital set up at nearby Kitebrook. 'Lending' Jessie in this way was part of May Richardson's contribution to the war effort. Jessie was keen on bowls, and was a lifelong member of the Congregational Church.[35]

Kitebrook VAD Hospital, originally located at Abbotswood in Stow-on-the-Wold, moved to Kitebrook House near Moreton-in-Marsh at the beginning of 1916. The house was lent by Mr and Mrs Freer. The photographs of the time show that the patients were accommodated in a large ward on the first floor (see Figures 16 and 17). The average number of resident patients was around 40.

By April 1918, bed numbers had increased to 70, all of which were full at the time of the Armistice. The Commandant at

17 *The main ward at Kitebrook Hospital, with the matron and a nurse in the centre of the picture.*

Kitebrook was a Mrs Pritchard MBE, and the Superintendent was Miss O'Donoghue. Just over 1,000 patients passed through the hospital during the war; most stayed no longer than about 40 days.[36]

May assisted the Red Cross, in a major way, in her role as Assistant Quartermaster at the Kitebrook VAD Hospital. She was well placed to utilise her extensive network of local friends to secure donations of money, food, cigarettes, games, promises of free transport and activities such as drives for the servicemen. Medical supplies also had to be collected from nearby VAD depots, transported and stored effectively, ready for instant use if needed.

The Government only paid just over three shillings a day per serviceman, and this was insufficient to cover the Hospital's costs. Apart from the type of donations listed above, fund raising through events such as garden fetes and musical recitals was also undertaken. The serviceman assisted in this process. For example, Privates Fairlie and Whitewell, from the Hospital, performed at a

18 *Senior staff and soldiers at Kitebrook VAD Hospital. Annie O'Donoghue, Robina Brown and Evelyn Fakes are the three nurses seated in the centre of the picture.*

whist drive, tea and entertainment at the Mann Institute in Moreton-in-Marsh, to assist the fundraising effort.

The VAD hospitals were attached to Central Military Hospitals. In many cases, women in the local neighbourhood volunteered on a part-time basis, as did local doctors (see Annex 3). Some paid workers, such as cooks, were also employed. The patients at the VAD hospitals were less seriously wounded than at full military hospitals, often needing only a period of convalescence. Figure 19 shows patients at Kitebrook enjoying a fete organised for their benefit by the local staff. Their headgear and cap badges show that they were from a number of different regiments. The VAD regime was less strict than, and the patients were not as crowded, as in full military hospitals. There were some three hundred VAD hospitals nationally, and 30 in Gloucestershire alone.

In an unusual arrangement, Evelyn Mary Brick was the stand-in butler at Chastleton from 1914 to 1918. She declined to stay on after the Great War, despite being asked to by May. Gordon, the

19 *A garden fete at Kitebrook VAD Hospital.*

head groom before the war, returned and took up the job of chauffeur. His war experiences had affected his health, and he felt unable to carry on the physically more demanding job of groom.

Richard Francis Richardson and the Battle of Loos

As with most families at the time, tragedy was never far away. CTR's nephew, Lieutenant Richard Francis Richardson (RR7), was the son of the Reverend Edward Taswell Richardson, vicar of Moreton Morrell in Warwickshire. Edward was CTR's younger brother and, as with other Richardson family members, RR7 was recorded in the 1911 Census as a student at Marlborough College (Figure 20). Joining the Army as a regular soldier, he was a second lieutenant, then lieutenant, in the 2nd Battalion of the Royal Warwickshire Regiment.[37]

RR7 was part of the British Expeditionary Force and embarked to the war in October 1914. He survived the first Battle of Ypres, but was injured at the lesser-known battle of Le Mesnil in

20 *Lieutenant Richard Francis Richardson, in the uniform of the Royal Warwickshire Regiment, 1914.*

December 1914. Here the regiment was ordered to take a well defended set of German trenches in front of Le Mesnil, which looked down on the British positions. His injuries (details unknown) were serious enough to keep him away from the regiment for eight months.

He only returned to duty on the 22nd August 1915. RR7 was then severely wounded on the first day of the Battle of Loos, just over a month later, on the 25th September 1915. He died five days later at Rouen, aged 21. Rouen had a large number of military hospitals; Richardson would have been transferred there by special hospital train.

The Battle of Loos, in a coal mining area south-west of Lille, was fought reluctantly by the British, largely at the behest of the French. The terrain was not favourable and the Germans had recently greatly reinforced their positions. Advancing in flat country west of Loos, the Warwickshires were virtually wiped out at the start of the battle. By the end of the first day, none of the 18 officers of the regiment were still standing, and only 140 men were left (there being 508 casualties among other ranks). In terms of men lost, this was one of the worst days of the whole war for the regiment. Figure 21 shows a typed extract of the original Warwickshire Regiment War Diary for the 25th September. This indicates, in a rather matter-of-fact way, that the attack started at 6.30am, with the German front and support trenches being taken early in the advance. It also records Richardson as wounded in action.

A soldier from the Royal Sussex Regiment, at the front that day, gives a graphic account of the scene:

> Dawn came on, misty and damp. We were to fire through the intensive bombardment just before the attack. At the given hour we started. The light was growing, and then one noticed little wisps of white smoke at close intervals along our line. These grew longer and spread, joined and formed a wall, blotting out the other side of the valley . . . The wall grew higher and higher, and drifted in rolls very slowly towards the German lines, not as a blank mist, but as a mass of rolling curls of smoke, stretching away, mile after mile . . . It was like a Doré illustration of some scene in Hell.[38]

The day is notable for the award of the first Victoria Cross obtained by the regiment in the Great War. Private Vickers cut the barbed wire in front of the German trenches, allowing the Warwickshires' advance towards the mining village of St Elie to continue.[39] Much of the land gained in the first day of the battle was subsequently lost, as the British reinforcements had been billeted too far to the rear to consolidate the gains made.

Chlorine gas was used here for the first time by the British, but with only moderate success. In some cases, British troops were affected by advancing through the gas they had released. It is not

IN TRENCHES.

24th   Wet Day. Casualties O.R. 3 wounded.

25th   5.50   Our bombardment ceased. Our advance
       a.m   commenced at 6.50 a.m. Took German
             front line trench then support
             trench then on to The Quarries as
             far as St. Elie. Captured about 60
     9.30   prisoners; arrived at this position
       a.m   at 9.30 a.m. Kept to it till after
             dark when we had to retire owing to
             the 9th Division on our left retiring.
     mid-   Occupied "Quarries" until midnight
   night.   when we took up a position in the
             communicating support trench 400
             yards west of the "Quarries". Up to
             this time the following officers were
             killed
             Lt Col B.P.Lefroy.D.S.O. (Died of
                                 wounds).

        Killed   Capt. H.H.L.Matear
                 Lieut F.R. Elderton
                      H.E. Edwards.
                 Lieut   J. Pennington.
                      J.S.O.Mansergh
             2 Lieut K.M. Gaunt
                      T.E. Newsome.

25th   and the following were <u>wounded</u>
(cont'd)

26th   Lt Col. B.P. Lefroy D.S.O.
             Capt. J.P. Duke
                   L.R. Swinhoe
                   J.S. Knyvett
            Lieut. R.F. Richardson
          2 Lieut. B.G. Hill
                   S.W.W.Cannon.
                   H. Allen.
                   E.W. Blenkinsop.
                   P.H. Diener.

      Missing. 2 Lieut. P.H.W. Herbage.

      Other Ranks :- Killed   64
                   Wounded 171
                   Missing 273

      The Battalion could only muster
      officer and 140 men.

21 *The first day of the Battle of Loos as recorded by the Royal Warwickshire Regiment War Diary; Richardson is listed as wounded at this stage.*

known whether Richardson was one of those who suffered this way, as no hospital records exist. He is most likely to have been killed by machine gun or rifle fire in what was an unusually flat and open battlefield. After a battle judged a debacle by many, General French was sacked and replaced by General Haig.[40]

Walter Seymour Carson and mini submarines

Charles Taswell Richardson's oldest daughter, Violet Taswell Richardson, was married to Walter Seymour Carson in September 1916. Walter's father, Edward Carson, had wanted WSC to go into the legal profession, but he joined the Navy instead and made a career there. Although it was at first difficult for Walter to communicate with his father, they later formed a close relationship during the Great War, when Walter won Edward's admiration for serving in the tiny and dangerous two-man submarines.[41]

Walter (WSC) had joined the Navy in 1912, and volunteered for submarines in 1914. Figure 22 shows him in his Navy uniform with his sister Aileen and brother Harry. At the time of his marriage, WSC was serving in HMS *Titania*, a submarine depot ship moored in Blyth Harbour, Northumberland. *Titania* provided supplies and accommodation for submarines and their crews (Figure 23). The officers had cabins on board, and other ranks were quartered in the town. From Blyth, the submarines patrolled the North Sea looking for German shipping.[42] Mini submarines at this time were regarded as 'death traps', being petrol and paraffin driven and highly unreliable.

Carson received glowing accounts of his personal and leadership qualities throughout his naval career, which lasted until 1934. Following his transfer to submarines, he was promoted to lieutenant, and completed further submarine training in 1915. His service record is exemplary. In 1916 he was judged 'a very keen and capable officer, highly spoken of by his captain as being thoroughly reliable in every way' (Captain Willes). In 1922 he was

22 *Walter Seymour Carson sitting behind his brother Harry and sister Aileen. He is in the uniform of a second lieutenant.*

23 HMS Titania, *the ship to which Walter Carson was assigned in 1916. The mini submarines are shown moored next to the depot ship.*

regarded as 'a very charming young man who should go far' (Captain Kiddle).[43]

Following the Great War, Carson was stationed for a number of years in the Far East. During this period his two daughters, Annette and Morwena, had some of their early education at Chastleton House, where they were accompanied by their nanny.

Carson was promoted to lieutenant-commander in 1922, and again received favourable reports from his superiors. Commander Ramsey, for example, rated him as 'a great assistance to me . . . very high sense of duty . . . handles officers and men well with firmness and tact . . . thoroughly reliable . . . good physique . . . keen on all games . . . leading hand in all entertainments'.[44] He was promoted to commander in 1927.

Edward Carson, Asquith and Northern Ireland

Walter Seymour Carson's father was Sir Edward Carson (EC). EC was one of the most famous barristers of the Edwardian period. He was born to a Protestant family in Dublin, and read Classics at Trinity College Dublin. Following a year reading Law, he was admitted to the Inns of Court in 1877.

He made his name as a barrister when he notably prosecuted in the Oscar Wilde homosexuality case. He was the champion of the Ulster Unionists at the height of their resistance to Irish Home Rule (Figure 24). Carson was the first person to sign the Ulster Covenant in 1912, and helped organise the Ulster Volunteer Force. He was one of the few commoners to have a state funeral when he died in 1935.[45]

Edward Carson was Attorney General in the Asquith-led Coalition Government in 1915. He played a significant role, however, in the removal of Asquith from his post in 1916, wishing to promote a more effective system of control for, and daily management of, the war. Just after Violet's September marriage at Chastleton, Carson resigned from the Government on the 19th

24 *Sir Edward Carson addresses an anti-Home Rule for Ireland rally.*

October 1916. This was planned in co-operation with Lloyd George and Bonar Law. He then became First Lord of the Admiralty in the replacement Lloyd George Government of December 1916.

Walter Seymour Carson was the youngest son of Edward's first marriage. The oldest son, William, was a spendthrift. Edward Carson bought him a farm in Kenya, but he was always in debt and had to be bailed out by his father. Carson called his children 'a rum lot'.[46]

WSC later lived, with Violet, at the Manor House, Stretton-on-Fosse, seven miles from Chastleton. He died of carbon monoxide gas poisoning in 1945 at an address in Jermyn Street, Piccadilly.

Rosemary Taswell Richardson and the Women's Royal Air Force

The Women's Royal Air Force (WRAF) was founded on the 1st April 1918 by the merger of the Women's Auxiliary Corps and the Women's Royal Naval Service. The minimum age for recruits was 18 years old. Rosemary Richardson joined the WRAF four weeks after its formation on the 28th April 1918, at the age of 18 years and eight months. On her RAF enrolment form she agreed to serve 'for the duration of the War'. Rosemary's medical assessment stated she was 'fit and well'.[47]

Rosemary was attached to 35 Training Squadron RAF, based at Portmeadow Aerodrome, Oxford. This squadron had moved from Northolt in December 1917. At this time WRAF personnel were divided into three groupings: Officers, Subordinate Officers and, rather curiously, Members. Rosemary was a Member within this classification (Figure 25).

Members comprised four categories: Clerical, Household, Technical and General. Rosemary was appointed, within the Technical category, as a 'Qualified driver on general duties – category C'.[48] The job involved an element of maintenance of the vehicle as well as driving, but in National Trust interviews, Rosemary noted that the car 'didn't break down' in her time, so the issue of her skill as a mechanic did not arise!

At this time the uniform was light khaki, rather than the subsequent blue of the RAF. Contemporary photographs show female drivers with a long skirt, shirt and tie, jacket with large lapels and patch pockets, leather gloves, and a floppy cap to complete the ensemble (Figure 26). Standing orders included uniform requirements and a ban on smoking on duty and in the street.[49]

The WRAF was also split into two further categories: 'mobiles' and 'immobiles'. Mobiles were prepared to serve anywhere at home or overseas. Rosemary joined as an immobile. These members were attached to their nearest station and were workers

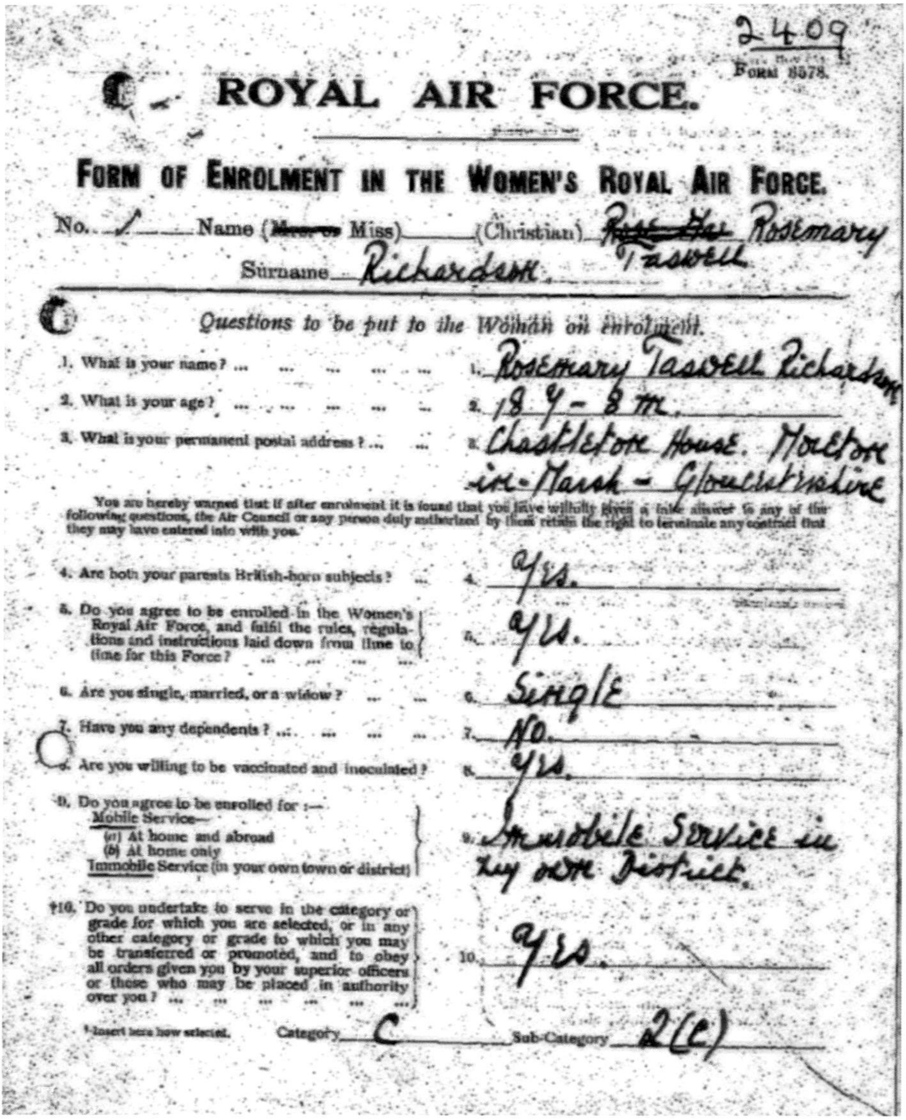

2409

FORM 8578.

ROYAL AIR FORCE.

FORM OF ENROLMENT IN THE WOMEN'S ROYAL AIR FORCE.

No. 1 Name (~~Mrs. or~~ Miss) (Christian) Rosemary Taswell

Surname Richardson.

Questions to be put to the Woman on enrolment.

1. What is your name? ... 1. Rosemary Taswell Richardson
2. What is your age? ... 2. 18 y – 8 m.
3. What is your permanent postal address? ... 3. Chastleton House. Moreton-in-Marsh – Gloucestershire

You are hereby warned that if after enrolment it is found that you have wilfully given a false answer to any of the following questions, the Air Council or any person duly authorized by them retain the right to terminate any contract that they may have entered into with you.

4. Are both your parents British-born subjects? ... 4. Yes.
5. Do you agree to be enrolled in the Women's Royal Air Force, and fulfil the rules, regulations and instructions laid down from time to time for this Force? ... 5. Yes.
6. Are you single, married, or a widow? ... 6. Single
7. Have you any dependents? ... 7. No.
8. Are you willing to be vaccinated and inoculated? 8. Yes.
9. Do you agree to be enrolled for:— Mobile Service— (a) At home and abroad (b) At home only Immobile Service (in your own town or district) 9. Immobile Service in my own District.
†10. Do you undertake to serve in the category or grade for which you are selected, or in any other category or grade to which you may be transferred or promoted, and to obey all orders given you by your superior officers or those who may be placed in authority over you? ... 10. Yes.

†Insert here how selected. Category C Sub-Category 2(c)

25 *Rosemary's enrolment form for the WRAF.*

26 *The uniform of a chauffeuse in the WRAF in 1918.*

who travelled to that base each day. Rosemary took lodgings (she termed them 'digs') in Wolvercote and cycled to the aerodrome each day. Rosemary 'kept her long hair' during this time.[50]

The job of the squadron was to train pilots before they were deployed to France or Belgium for action at the front. Some of the pilots at Portmeadow came from Canada and the USA, (as well as Czarist Russia), as these countries were increasingly involved in the war.[51]

This was a time of fast-moving growth and change in the RAF, with airmen moving into training squadrons, and then on to deployment in operational situations. The government set up the School of Military Aeronautics at Oxford University, requisitioning premises from eight Oxford colleges for the purpose. Following training here, or at the other centre at Reading University, recruits undertook operational flying training at a base such as Portmeadow. Canadian pilots had a similar procedure, initially training in Ontario before carrying out advanced work in the UK before deployment.[52] Annexe 4 gives more details of the attitudes and exploits of one Canadian pilot trained at Portmeadow.

Portmeadow Aerodrome

The grass airfield, a temporary facility, was originally set up on the northern edge of Portmeadow in 1911, and was used for military training purposes. The airfield covered 260 acres, and the buildings included a semi-permanent hangar-cum-workshop measuring 250 feet by 90 feet, a large number of timber huts, bell tents and, by May 1918, seven canvas hangars.

An access road was built into the northern part of the site, permission for which was granted in 1916. The French-made *Bessonneau* canvas hangars were capable of being erected in 48 hours. When used in Northern France, they allowed the air squadrons to move base quickly to follow changes in the front line (Figure 27).

Despite the activities of the Royal Flying Corps and the RAF, the site remained common grazing land. The first job every morning was to drive the cattle off the airfield, before flying could begin!

For training purposes the outline of an aeroplane was laid out on the meadow, in chalk rocks, as a target for air-to-ground firing (Figure 28). Also, a small concrete building called 'the target' was erected on the edge of Wolvercote Common, and ground crew used this to shelter after erecting temporary targets. The flyers would then release bags of flour, by hand, over the side of the open cockpits of their aircraft to practise bombing.

The aeroplanes flown were Avro 504s, Sopwith Pups and

27 *Portmeadow Aerodrome Oxford. The camouflage on the front of the* Bessonneau *temporary hangars on the right of the picture can be clearly seen. The photograph was taken on the 31st May 1918, during Rosemary's period of service.*

28 *The air-to-ground target at Portmeadow. This was made up of chalk stones to represent the body of a plane and crossed planks to represent the swastika markings.*

Camels and, during Rosemary's time, Bristol F2b fighters (Figure 29). The airfield was closed in early 1919, and Rosemary concluded her period of service.[53] Flying activities at this time were very dangerous, and there were at least six crashes at the aerodrome, or in the vicinity, amounting to the loss of 13 lives. Ten of these airmen's graves lie in Wolvercote Cemetery in North Oxford.[54]

29 *A Bristol F2b fighter plane at Portmeadow in 1918.*

CHAPTER 3

The end of an era?

Mysterious death at sea

After the Great War, Charles Taswell Richardson travelled by sea to India to inspect his tea estates. Returning from Calcutta, he embarked on the 4th February 1920 on the SS *City of Marseilles*. The ship was especially built for the Indian trade, with a high proportion of first class cabins and a special ventilation system for the hot weather (Figure 30). The ship also had a native curry cook, who would initiate western passengers into the largely unfamiliar Indian dishes on their way to and from India.[55]

30 *Charles Taswell Richardson left Calcutta on the SS City of Marseilles on the 4th February 1920.*

Charles drowned seven days later on the 11th February 1920. The *Register of Births, Marriages and Deaths at Sea* gives the cause of death as 'disappearance at sea'. This would suggest that he had gone overboard from the ship, rather than succumbing to a tropical disease, and then being buried at sea.[56]

The location of CTR's death is given as 14.12N 85.45E, in the Bay of Bengal, halfway between Calcutta and Ceylon (see Figure 31). This is broadly on the same latitude as Madras (Chennai).

The journey to Sylhet (then in India), where his plantations were located, would have been an onerous one for Richardson, well into his sixth decade. The three-month sea voyage was only the precursor to an uncomfortable 30-or-more-day journey on the small native steamer which traversed the Brahmaputra River, and its tributaries in the rainy season, from Calcutta. The area was notorious for the number of deaths experienced by previous British tea planters. Problems included high temperatures, and the extreme humid climate, with diseases such as malaria, cholera, kala-azar (the parasite disease also called 'black fever'), small pox, dysentery and typhoid being widespread.

Passengers like Richardson would typically be quartered in a single cabin on a barge towed by a steamer. The journey could offer a range of occurrences to enliven the voyage for the tea planter. The steamer would frequently run aground on one or more of the sandbanks along the river. If a rifle was to hand, there was the chance of a shot at wild buffalo or the ducks that flew overhead. When the boat moored up each night, the tea planter could go ashore and meet other planters who had come to the landing place to buy extra provisions, such as tins of salmon, cigars, brandy and beer from the steamer captain.

Such steamers would also carry large numbers of what the Edwardians called 'coolies' (often tea workers) travelling as deck passengers, and bound for the various tea gardens. At every landing place they would rush ashore to buy eggs, vegetables, chickens and even goats, which contributed to the general air of uproar and

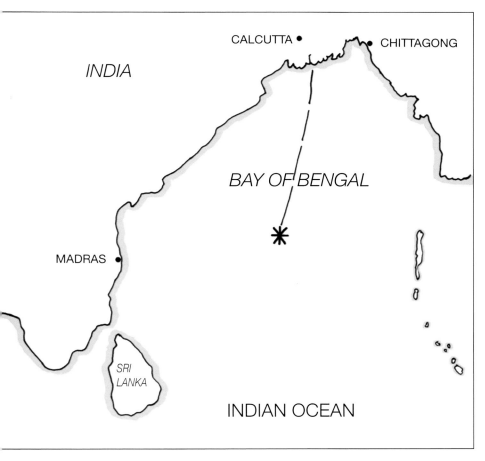

31 *Location of Charles Taswell Richardson's drowning in the Bay of Bengal, 1920.*

32 *Local steamer on the Brahmaputra River.*

disorganisation aboard. Figure 32 shows a paddle steamer of the era towing an accommodation barge, or 'flat' as it was called.[57]

The value of Richardson's will was £64,000, the equivalent of £2,880,000 at current monetary values.[58] May Richardson was to receive a lump sum of £1,000 to pay immediate expenses, and the income from half of the estate for her life, with the income from the remainder being put into trust for the children until they reached 21 years of age. May was one of three trustees for the will, the others being Richard Taswell Richardson (Uncle Dick), and the family solicitor, William Horton of Bennetts Hill, Birmingham.

The result was that, for the remainder of the tenancy, May was head of the household with two daughters, until 1931, when the number went down to one upon Rosemary's wedding. House improvements and other activities, however, did not abate.

On the home front

The house provided a base for hunting in the Cotswolds and, in the later years of the tenancy, members of the family, especially Rosemary and Veronica, rode to hounds.[59] The Richardson family had a number of hunt friends in the Chipping Norton and Moreton-in-Marsh areas, as well as at Snowshill Manor, near Broadway. Social life revolved around the Heythrop and North Cotswold Hunts, with Colonel Alexander, Rosemary's eventual husband, recounting an anecdote about a hunt ball on the tapes.[60]

Staying in the Cavalier Room on the first floor, Colonel Alexander could not find his uniform for the Hunt Ball, which should have been laid out for him by one of the servants. Following a trip to the 'nether regions' (the servants' quarters in the basement) to enquire of its whereabouts, it transpired the uniform had been laid out in the Secret Room, next to the Cavalier Room and above the front entrance lobby of the house. This was only accessible by pressing on a barely identifiable wallpapered panel in the corner of the room.

May Richardson carried out further improvements to the house including the installation of water tanks in the roof and other water supply and drainage works, some relating to the Dairy Court. Decorations and wallpapering were also carried out around this time (which was only a few months after the death of CTR). In 1920, Messrs Gray, the same builders as used before the Great War, estimated £95 for rubbing down and re-painting walls in the west staircase, and wallpapering some of the adjacent corridors.

Electricity and heating was extended to further parts of the house. In 1920, Gray again quoted, this time the sum of £245, for the work involving the installation of ten radiators in the porch, the Screens Passage, the Oak Parlour and the Great Hall (Figure 33). An electric bell system had been installed near the Butler's Pantry on the ground floor, and on the third floor landing near the servants' rooms, earlier in the Richardsons' tenancy.[61]

From **GEORGE H. GRAY,**

Builder and Decorator,

MORETON-IN-MARSH.

Specification and Estimate for proposed work to be done

at *Chastleton House*

for *Mrs Richardson*

Aug 12 1920

Supply & fix 4 Radiators viz one in The White
Parlour one in The Dining room one in The
Young Ladies' room & one in the maids' room of
suitable size for the rooms.
Remove & rearrange the pipes to Dining room
to ensure a good circulation
Remove & replace with larger the pipes for the
service to Young Ladies' & maids' rooms
Remove present Boiler & Stack & replace
with New Sectional Boiler of sufficient
capacity for the whole of The Radiators
alter the main flow & return pipes to
present Boiler & fix them lower to give a
better rise from New Boiler
The whole to be carried out in a satisfactory
manner & left in good working order for
the sum of Two Hundred & forty five
Pounds nett cash on completion

£245—0—0

Geo H Gray

33 *Quotation from Messrs Gray, builders, for central heating work.*

The Richardsons had a real interest in the garden, creating new planting and borders near the topiary in the Best Garden. This reflected the fashion of the time for lots of bold colour in gardens. The previous beech hedge surrounding the topiary was rooted out and replaced with yew (see Figure 34). Four new arches were created and planted with vines and roses; a paper bark maple (*acer griseum*) was also planted north of the topiary. Figure 35 shows that by 1936 there were extensive herbaceous borders near the topiary. The indication is that the topiary and its surrounding yew hedge were both smaller than they are today.

At around this time a natural Wilderness and Nuttery Garden was created, following the precepts of the fashionable garden designer William Robinson. It comprised an informal path weaving

34 *Topiary planting in the Best Garden at Chastleton House.*

through a wooded area at the northern end of the main garden, with many ground cover plants such as anemonies, *tulipa sylvestris* and bluebells. This formed part of a peripheral path round the garden.

A new wall, border and steps were created on the North Terrace; this separated the upper part of the terrace from the croquet and tennis lawns, and gave a more formal feel to this part of the garden. A thatched rustic building was located south of the tennis court and is shown on photographs of the time (Figure 3). A greenhouse, situated on the western side of the house, remained in use. There was also a hotbed for growing exotic fruit. As the National Trust Handbook states, 'the garden rose to new horticultural heights' during the Richardson era.[62]

35 *The Topiary Garden and herbaceous borders form an attractive background for this garden fete at Chastleton.*

The daily routine

The details of the post-war daily routine at Chastleton can be assembled from tapes of interviews with servants, and from other sources. The layout of the servants' domain, the basement, at Chastleton shows some seven main spaces, including a large cellar (Figure 36).

According to the tapes, housemaids had a constant round of duties: they made up early morning trays, drew the blinds and tidied rooms 'all the time'. They changed for dinner and, in the evening, turned beds down and inserted hot water bottles. The kitchen maid kept a fire going to provide kettles of hot water at any time. The main staircase had to be polished, and floor scrubbing started from the front door. There was lots of dusting.

Female servants were not provided with uniforms, (print dress, black stockings and cap), but had the right to have one dress washed by the laundry per week. The cook dressed in white. The laundry was done in Chastleton village, at 'Townsend's cottage', about 200 yards from the main house. The laundry maids went up to the house for their lunches each day.

Meat was purchased during the 1920s from the Co-operative Society in Chipping Norton. May would put £10 'behind the counter', with the costs of individual orders being taken from the deposited sum. The meat order cost around £1 a week. Very little was wasted during cooking: cold meat was used for supper, bones were put in a stock pot, and soup was produced. Jacket potatoes, rissoles and cottage pies were regularly made. Breadcrumbs were made by putting the loaves through sieves. Horseradish sauce, with cream, was also handmade.

The family had four horses at maximum. The Head Groom and Assistant Groom were located in rooms adjacent to the stables. During the Richardsons' time, the Brewhouse was used as a store, particularly for garden materials.

The most recent Chastleton House Guidebook suggests

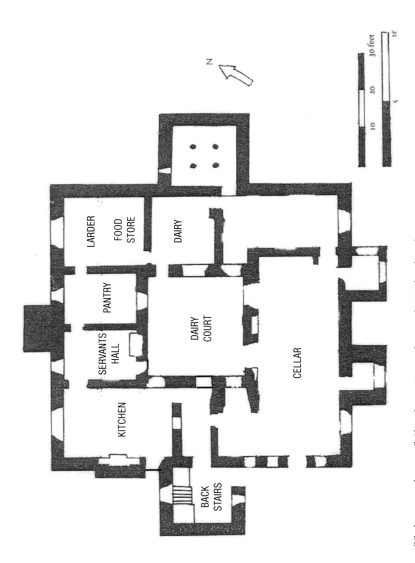

36 *Layout of 'below stairs' area of Chastleton House during the Richardsons' time.*

there were 19 staff made up of '11 indoor servants and eight outdoor staff' during the 1920s. The tapes of Dorothy Hadland's recollections of the early 1930s indicate there were 14 staff made up of:

- nine indoor servants: a butler, parlour maid, hall boy-footman; three kitchen staff (including the cook), three housemaids and a nanny; and
- five outdoor staff: Head Gardener, second and third gardeners, a chauffeur and a groom.[63]

At this time the cook was paid £1 a week, and the housemaids 50p a week.

The profile of servants after the Great War was different from that before, in a number of significant respects. The pre-war servants were generally from a distance away from Chastleton, and recruited through agencies that ran 'registry offices'. The Richardsons used one such facility in Witney to recruit Dorothy Hadland, who had originally lived in Devon. Some authors suggest that this reduced the urge by servants to return home regularly, and thus kept their focus on their jobs.[64] After the war, servants were more difficult to find, and a greater proportion came from the local area. There was probably also a higher turnover of servants at this time.

The different figures for servant numbers suggest consider-able 'coming and going' of staff during the Richardson period, and it was likely there was some difficulty in retaining staff. The taped interviews suggest that working in the depth of the Cotswold countryside was very quiet, and some servants, partic-ularly the younger ones, may have suffered from boredom as a result. As one stated, 'the hours were long, but the work was not very hard'.

The daily routine rarely varied. The kitchen maid would light the kitchen fire each day at 6.00am. Kindling from the garden would be left next to the kitchen door by the under gardener, 'young Skelcher'. Coffee would then be taken up to the cook in her room on the third floor. Blacking of the grate in the kitchen was a daily job.

By 8.00am breakfast had to be ready for the family. At 9.00am, breakfast and other food was taken to the nursery. The house had 47 candles, each of which had to be trimmed daily. This was done by the hall boy-footman.

At the beginning of the week, May Richardson would come down to the kitchen and discuss with the cook the numbers and type of visitors expected, and the food required. The family kept two cows. The under gardener would milk the cows. The top of the milk would be skimmed off for cream, and some of the rest would be churned for butter. The hand churn was very tedious, and butter-making took 'a very long time' according to Mrs Hadland! Much use was made of produce from the garden, with jams and preserves being produced. Attempts to preserve carrots were made one year, but these failed.

Lunch would be at 1.00pm, followed by activities such as croquet or tennis. Shopping for clothes was something done infrequently, perhaps three or four times a year. Dinner was scheduled for 7.45pm. The pantry boy waited at table, taking the food up from the basement.

Colonel Alexander, in a taped interview, noted that Chastleton was 'a lovely house, full of cheerful people', and that there was 'a happy atmosphere'. After dinner the family sometimes played hide and seek: 'there were lots of cupboards to hide in', and the games 'went on a long time'.[65]

At Christmas there were rarely large parties, although a Christmas tree was erected in the hall. Presents were given by the Richardsons to the servants. These were often 'useful' items, such as a woollen coat or material for making a nightdress.

In the late 1920s, card playing with small groups of invited guests became a popular pursuit of May Richardson. The cook claimed Mrs Richardson's mood in the morning would betray how well she had done at cards the previous evening!

Although the Long Gallery was called the Ballroom on some plans of the house, it was not used for this purpose. It was only ever full during the Richardson era for whist drives, perhaps two or three a year, the proceeds of which were donated to the local cottage hospitals in Moreton-in-Marsh and Chipping Norton, or to the Red Cross.

The Great Hall was occasionally used as a ballroom. A ball organised during the winter of 1927 was called off due to a major snowstorm. Mrs Hadland recalls the servants enjoyed eating through the food that had been prepared for the guests for a number of days!

May Richardson was well liked in Chastleton village. As Mrs Hadland the kitchen maid, referring to the late 1920s, put it, 'the village loved her'. She loaned Violet's wedding dress to the daughter of one of the farm tenants for her wedding. She raised money for good causes, and supported local efforts such as collections for the voluntary hospital established at nearby Kitebrook during the Great War. May would arrange for any villager who was ill to be taken to the doctor.

In the later years she was happy to let servants go to the cinema in Moreton-in-Marsh. Rosemary would also go to the cinema with friends as she states 'as a rag' or 'for a lark'. Her taped comments suggest that she thought it was not a very good picture house.

The Playhouse Cinema was located in the rear yard of the Manor House Hotel in Church Street, Moreton-in-Marsh. It opened in 1927, and had seating for just over 350 filmgoers, all on a single level. The curved roof remains today, and has a number of prominent ventilators, as shown in Figure 37. The cinema closed in 1966.

37 *The Playhouse Cinema, Moreton-in-Marsh.*

Augustus Alexander and the Central India Horse

Rosemary married Augustus Gordon Stewart Alexander (AGSA) at Chastleton in 1931. AGSA was born in 1899 and was educated at Marlborough School. He was the son of a doctor who had purchased a practice in Broadway some 10 years before.

Rosemary's wedding was impressive, with a large number of guests, as Figures 39 and 40 show. A special picnic was put on in the stable yard for Chastleton residents and those visiting from the groom's property in Broadway (Figure 42).

At the age of 17 years and 11 months Rosemary's husband had left school, entering Quetta Command and Staff College (then in India) as a cadet. Quetta was the most prestigious training institution in the Indian Army, and had been established in 1905 by Lord Kitchener. Field Marshalls Waverley, Montgomery, Auchinleck and Slim had previously trained there.[66]

After passing out, AGSA was commissioned as a second lieutenant in the Central India Horse. The Central India Horse had first

38 *Rosemary Taswell Richardson escorted to the church for her wedding by Commander The Hon.Walter Carson.*

39 *Guests at the wedding of Rosemary Taswell Richardson to Augustus Alexander, 1931.*

40 *Throwing confetti as the couple leave on honeymoon; Rosemary's wedding.*

41 *Rosemary's favourite hunter 'greets' the bride after the wedding. The two bridesmaids are Veronica Taswell Richardson and Katrine Alexander, the sister of the bridegroom.*

been raised as an irregular cavalry regiment during the Indian Mutiny of 1857. The regiment, which had English officers leading Indian troops, was involved in the Egyptian Expeditionary Force, originally sent to protect the Suez Canal in 1917, and in the Palestinian Campaign of 1917–18.

The 38th Central India Horse, Alexander's regiment, was part of the 4th Cavalry Division created in August 1918 as part of the reorganisation of the Egyptian Expeditionary Force for the Palestine offensive. The offensive, commencing in late September 1918, involved attacking and breaking through the Turkish defences on the coastal plain of what is now Gaza and Haifa, and cutting off any Turkish retreat further north, a cavalry drive of over 50 miles. This engagement, the Battle of Megiddo, was the last major battle where cavalry was of decisive importance in war. The cavalry pushed on and entered Damascus on October 1st, reaching Aleppo by the 25th of the month. The speed and comprehensiveness of this victory, contrasting with the static position in the trenches on the Western Front, was praised by General Allenby, who was in charge of the troops.[67]

AGSA was stationed at the Central India Horse base/depot in Gwalior, India, during 1918, and although placed on notice to go to Palestine, did not arrive before the war ended. As a 19-year-old he was the only British officer left at the base in late 1918. With his Indian officers he was in charge of 1,500 men and nearly 1,000 horses. A major part of his job was to train and prepare re-enforcements and despatch them safely to Palestine.[68] After the war it was six years before he came back to England, but, as an aide-de-camp to the Viceroy Lord Irwin, he would have represented a good 'catch' for Rosemary with the country denuded of eligible young men.

In India, Alexander was able to live a life resembling that of an English squire. With servants and cooks to do the chores, he would hunt or shoot, as well as playing polo with the regimental teams. An occasional foray onto the streets to confront opposition from local nationalists seems not to have worried him: 'they tended to melt away when they knew we were coming,' he states in one interview.[69]

This lifestyle also suited Rosemary when she went to India after her marriage. She loved the country, even noting it had electricity where she was living, in contrast to Chastleton, where the predominant form of illumination remained the candle!

After retirement, Alexander worked as an official at the Hurlingham Club in London. Hurlingham was the headquarters of polo for the British Empire from 1874 until the Second World War. The Hurlingham polo ground was compulsorily purchased by the London County Council after the Second World War, and developed for housing.

42 *A picnic for villagers and staff at Rosemary's wedding, held in the stable yard at Chastleton House. Dorothy Hadland, one of the kitchen servants, is holding a cup of tea in the second row, and is wearing a black hat. The children on the front row are l to r: Enid Skelcher, Florrie Newman, Joan Skelcher and Doris Skelcher.*

43 *Locals looking over the wall of the churchyard at the wedding. Chastleton Church is in the background.*

Arthur Taylor and the founding of Lloyds Bank

Less is known about CTR's youngest daughter, Veronia. She went to school at Bedgebury Park (Kent) from age 13, and was an enthusiatic member of the Hethrop and North Cotswold hunts. The North Cotswold is centred on Broadway, and it is likely she met her future husband, Arthur Taylor, through this hunting connection. Veronica married Taylor in 1933 in Chastleton Church. Irene Whitmore Jones gave them permission to hold the reception at Chastleton House (Figure 44).

Arthur Taylor (1902–1971) was a landowner and farmer in Worcestershire. His father had owned estates in Moseley and Yardley, Birmingham. At the time he married, Taylor lived at Bibsworth House in Broadway, an Arts and Crafts style house built in 1904 by Guy Dawber, a well known Cotswold architect (Figure 45).

44 *The bridal party at Veronica Taswell Richardson's wedding. Annette and Morwena Carson are the two bridesmaids on the left of the photograph, and May Taswell Richardson is standing to their left in the dark dress.*

45 *Bibsworth House, Broadway, home of Arthur Taylor and Veronica Taswell Richardson.*

Pevsner, the architectural historian, describes the design of Bibsworth House as Dawber 'at his most Lutyenesque' (that is, reflecting the work of one of the best-known architects of the time, Edward Lutyens). Dawber worked in Lutyens' office for a short while in the 1890s. Among his other commissions was the post office in Broadway, Eyford Park in Upper Slaughter, and Burdocks in Fairford.[70]

During his career, Dawber was clerk of works at Batsford Park for Lord Redesdale, acted as President of the Royal Institute of British Architects from 1925–7, and was prominent in the founding of the Council for the Preservation of Rural England in 1926.

Arthur's most well known ancestor was John Taylor, who was one of the most prominent manufacturers in Birmingham at the start of the eighteenth century. He made his fortune making gilt buttons in the 1730s.

Taylor also brought 'japanning', a form of varnishing, to Birmingham, using it on items such as snuff boxes, belt buckles and vinaigrettes. At the peak of the business in the 1740s, five hundred persons were employed in his factory in Crooked Lane, Dale End in central Birmingham. He promoted the division of labour, with his buttons passing through the hands of many operatives, each with a defined task. Many of his employees were women, some working from home. He was even visited by Dr Samuel Johnson, who was fascinated by the industries of Birmingham. His collaborator Boswell called Taylor one of Johnson's 'valuable' acquaintances.[71]

In 1765, recognising the need for finance to start businesses, John Taylor set up a bank with his neighbour Sampson Lloyd II, (a Quaker). This initially traded as Taylor and Lloyd. The firm eventually became the Lloyds Bank of today. In its early years, the bank gave loans to companies such as those run by Matthew Boulton and James Watt. John Taylor's son, John II, built Moseley Hall which had grounds landscaped by Humphrey Repton.[72]

John Taylor II invested his large profits in land, purchasing over

1,000 acres in Yardley on the southern edge of the city. In 1913, this was then sold to Birmingham Corporation for housing, following the introduction of the Town Planning Act of 1909 which allowed local authorities to make development schemes. The proceeds of this would have made his son Arthur extremely wealthy. Arthur then moved further out from the city, purchasing Strensham Hall in Worcestershire as his country residence.

Reflections

The Richardsons were a resourceful family. Starting as trade apprentices, they rose to being a prominent merchant family in Chester. With their finances more secure, having diversified successfully also into mining, they entered the landowning classes with the purchase of an estate at Capenhurst. A close involvement in local politics and affairs also typified the family, with successive generations serving as deputy lieutenants and justices of the peace in Cheshire.

From the start of the nineteenth century family members moved into the traditional professions, with the law, the church, the military and engineering being most popular. Each generation saw large numbers of children being born, up to ten being the norm. This was a proud traditional family, with the same names cropping up through the generations: Richard, Charles, Thomas and William on the male side, and Annie, Louisa and Fanny on the female side.

Charles Taswell Richardson, who rented Chastleton, had inherited family wealth, but also appeared an astute businessman. Where many speculators had lost money in the Indian tea trade, his well-chosen connections helped him to survive and prosper. The reasons for his death at sea remain a mystery and require further research.

Chastleton appears an oasis of calm among the busy lives of the Richardsons. The family kept a full complement of servants, and was able to make improvements to both the house and garden. The

daughters seemed to live a happy existence among their contemporaries in North Oxfordshire. Links with the village and locality
were strong, with Charles and May doing a lot to help local people.

Reflecting their range of local contacts, the Richardson
daughters married into well connected and entrepreneurial middle
and upper class families. The Taylors in Birmingham had made their
fortune bringing the craft skill of japanning to England, and using
it for the production of 'toys' in Birmingham, a parallel perhaps to
the Richardson's goldsmithing enterprise and inventiveness in
Chester. The other sisters, Violet and Rosemary, married husbands
in the services. In each case the 'in-laws' were in the professions,
Seymour Carson's father being one of the most eminent lawyers of
the age, and Augustus Alexander's a well-regarded doctor who had
purchased a practice in Broadway.

The 37 years spent by the Richardsons at Chastleton were, on
the whole, successful ones. Charles was a respected local figure,
and May was both resilient and well liked. The house was well
maintained and improvements were made to the garden. The
family were connected to many of the great events of the time,
particularly in the Great War.

After Charles' death, May seems to have carried on with great
resolve and courage to make a friendly and happy home for her
daughters. It was only at the end of the 1920s that she was shedding
servants to save house-running costs. The lives of the Richardsons
give a fascinating glimpse into Victorian, Edwardian and Georgian
affairs, both in England and further afield.

Following the Richardsons' exit, the house was again advertised
for rent, but there were no takers. Irene Whitmore Jones moved
back in and attempted to keep the house going by opening it to
visitors. With little income she was forced to auction off more than
1,000 acres of land in 1936. Irene now lived alone in the house with
only a butler and a maid for company. The 'lovely House, full of
cheerful people', described by Rosemary's husband Augustus
Alexander, had come and gone. It truly was the end of an era.

Chastleton House room layout

Chastleton House faces south. The house is built around a courtyard named the Dairy Court. The Richardsons largely used the rooms on ground and first floors. The best rooms, used for entertaining and for showing the family's status, were located on the eastern side of the house.

Ground Floor

The Great Hall is a large open room with a wooden screen at the western end and a central hearth, typical of medieval houses. During the Richardsons' time this was used as a sitting room, with a circular table and easy chairs, evident in photographs taken by *Country Life* in 1902.

The White Parlour was May Richardson's favourite room. A fully panelled room, which had been painted white for a family wedding in the 1850s, it affords a view down the drive to observe visitors as they arrive. It was where May transacted family business, and received guests, as well as being used as a sitting room.

The Great Parlour was used by the Richardsons for main meals, such as the evening meal. It could be reached by servants from the basement by a staircase in the pantry.

The Oak Parlour had been used as an estate office by the Whitmore-Jones family, during the eighteenth century. It is likely this was used also as an office by the Richardsons.

The Butler's Pantry remained in use. Here the butler kept the glassware and silverware, and was able to monitor the front door.

The hall boy lived in a room next to the Butler's Pantry, on the ground floor, so that he could answer the front door bell. The bell system designed by the Richardsons can be found on the wall in the corridor outside the pantry.

The children's nursery was off the Great Parlour on the northern side of the Dairy Court.

Ground floor

First Floor

Here the important room was the Great Chamber, the most ornate room in the house. If a large group of visitors was being entertained, this would be where the guests would assemble before eating.

The Sheldon Room was where Charles and May had their bedroom. Other bedrooms on this floor, used by daughters or visitors, were the Cavalier and Fettiplace rooms.

First floor

Second Floor

The Long Gallery, running the full length of the northern side of the house, performed a role as a corridor for servants going to their bedrooms in rooms on the south side of the Dairy Court, near the Museum Room. The main use of the Long Gallery, during the Richardsons' time, was for events such as whist drives, organised to raise money for local charities.

Five of the indoor staff lived in two bedrooms at the top of the house. The cook had a room to herself, but four other staff shared another bedroom.

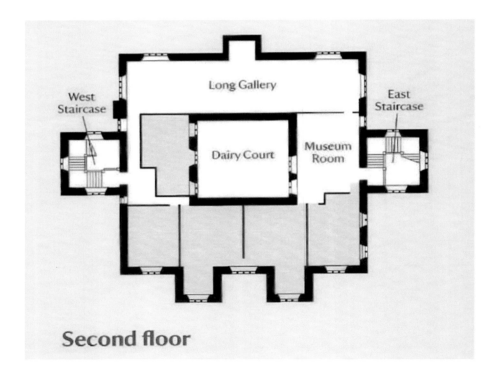

Second floor

Life below stairs

The downstairs rooms are arranged around an open Dairy Court (see Figure 36). In the late 1920s all of the below stairs rooms were still lit by lamps, which had to be trimmed daily. Ice was bought from the local shop and used in the dairy and food store, and salt was used as a preservative.

First room

This was the kitchen, where a new cooking range had been installed in 1885. There were sinks under the window on the northern wall, with a plate rack. There were two ovens, one used for cooking cakes and pastries, and the other for meat and roasts. The range used coal, and there was a coal bunker by the stove. The flues were cleaned out each week. There was a large table in the centre of the room, with one end covered in lead sheet to allow for the placing down of hot pans. Plates were stored in a cupboard to the right of the entrance door.

Second room

This was the Servants Hall. It had a table in the middle, a sofa along one wall and various cupboards. The butler sat at one end of the table and the cook at the other. The range was lit, and was used to warm the room. No cooking took place, although water could be heated upon it. A wireless was placed on a high shelf. This could be used only if a wireless in the Great Hall or White Parlour was also switched on by the family!

Third room

This was the pantry, where food was assembled before being carried up to the dining room. If the food was cold it would be kept on a table here. If hot, the hall boy would come down to the kitchen for the food to carry it up. The stairs in the corner of this room had been put in by the Whitmore-Joneses in the 1820s to make the service between the kitchen and Great Parlour more convenient.

Fourth room

This was the larder and general food store. Such rooms would normally be on the cooler northern side of the property, as here at Chastleton. There was a game box, with gauze sides, located on the west wall. There was a bread bin on the right of the door and a table in the middle of the room. There were hooks hanging from the ceiling for meat and ham, although these were not used in the 1920s and 1930s. Prepared food was also stored here. On one occasion the under gardener brought some ice in, but also relieved the larder of some rice puddings stored there! The butler would sometimes come downstairs at night. The cook felt he was looking to see if there was any leftover food, stored in the larder, which he could use for a midnight feast!

Fifth room

This was the dairy, with apparatus for making butter. Milk and cream was also stored here. There was direct access to this room across the Dairy Court. Cheese had been made here in the past, but was not made during the Richardsons' time.

Sixth room

This is the cellar, which has space for the storage of wine as well as beer. Barrels were no longer brought from the Brewhouse and rolled into the cellar. Beer was, by the time of the Richardsons' tenancy, delivered from outside breweries.

ANNEX 3

Kitebrook VAD Hospital

During the Great War, Voluntary Aided Detachment (VAD) hospitals were organised and administered by the Joint War Committee of the Red Cross Society and the Order of St John. VAD detachments were set up to fill the gaps in Territorial medical services. VAD volunteers needed to be 19–50 years old; and were subject to a one month probation period. If successful, they then had to commit to at least six months service. VAD hospitals received just over three shillings per day for each patient; this was often only about 80% of the money needed. Therefore the remainder had to be raised by the Hospitals, and/or the local Red Cross groups themselves.

For women who wanted to 'do something for the War effort', the VAD hospitals provided an outlet, helping the wounded from a range of overseas campaigns. The wives and daughters of land owners and professional families, living in North Oxfordshire and Gloucestershire, were attracted to the Kitebrook Hospital, as the listing below reveals.

Organisation

The Kitebrook VAD Hospital was organised jointly by the Moreton-in-Marsh and Stow-on-the-Wold detachments of the Red Cross Society. It had originally been located at Abbotswood near Stow-on-the-Wold, but had moved to Kitebrook House in 1916, the property being loaned by Mr and Mrs Freer.

Female detachments varied according to local conditions, but generally consisted of:

- A Commandant;
- A Medical Officer;
- A Quartermaster; and
- 22 women, of whom two were to be qualified nurses.

Detachments met at least monthly and worked towards first aid and home nursing qualifications.

Much of the basic work in VAD hospitals was the responsibility of the VADs (termed 'nursing members'). Their tasks included cleaning, scrubbing, dusting, setting trays, cooking breakfasts and lighting fires. They also helped dress, undress and wash the servicemen.

Paid staff

The staff list for Kitebrook, listed on the Red Cross Society website, indicates that the most senior medically-qualified person was Miss Anna O'Donoghue. She was the Matron, and effectively in charge of the day to day medical side. Miss O'Donoghue came from County Clare in Eire and was paid £54-12 shillings per annum salary.

Two Nursing Sisters were also employed. These were:

- Miss Robina Brown, from Cambridge, who was paid £64-12 shillings per annum;
- and Miss Evelyn Fakes, from Long Melford, Suffolk, who was paid an undisclosed sum by the Joint Committee.

The Hospital also employed Miss Winifred Drummond, under the title of 'massage and electrical'. Miss Drummond was paid £52-12 shillings per annum. Electric shock treatment was used in VAD hospitals to treat servicemen suffering from what would now be termed post-traumatic stress disorder.

Mr Mark Style was the Quartermaster for the Hospital, and Mrs C T Richardson was the Assistant Quartermaster.

Nursing Members

The Nursing Members carried out all of the medical, clearing and cleaning tasks listed above, including night duty. Among Nursing Members were:

- Mrs Margaret Henderson of Little Compton Manor. Captain Henderson was the owner of the Manor at the time;
- Mrs Mabel Cheetham, married to the owner of Eyford Park, Lower Slaughter. Eyford was designed by Guy Dawber in 1911, and was voted England's Favourite House by *Country Life* magazine in 2011;
- Miss Audrey Fenwick, daugher of the owner of Abbotswood, Stow-on-the-Wold;
- Mrs Florence Maxwell, of Cotswold House, Stow-on-the-Wold. Cotswold House is an impressive town house on the northern side of the Square in Stow-on-the-Wold, and is now occupied by an art gallery;
- Miss Susan Arkell, of Duncome, Moreton-in-Marsh;
- Mrs Florence Dening of Manor House, Stow-on-the-Wold;
- Miss Lorna Horseman-Bailey of Foxholes, Kingham; her brother, Major Guy Horseman, was awarded the MC in 1917;
- Miss Mary Bliss, of Croftdown, Witney;
- Mrs Gertrude Gibbs of High Street, Moreton-in-Marsh;
- Mrs Jane Hicks of Barton-on-the-Heath;
- Mrs Catherine Fisher of Barton-on-the-Heath, and
- Mrs Henrietta Fry of Longborough, Moreton-in-Marsh

(Source: www.redcross.org.uk/About-us/Who-we-are/History-and-origin/First-World-War)

ANNEX 4

A flavour of life in the Royal Flying Corps

These accounts give a flavour of the precariousness of life within the Royal Flying Corps and the RAF, and the way in which young pilots operated at the time. It covers three crashes, two on the edge of Oxford, and one in combat conditions.

Local accident – 1

The chief instructor of the squadron and another pilot were flying in to Portmeadow from Larkhill in Wiltshire, when their Bristol monoplane crashed short of the airfield in Wolvercote. The two pilots were named as Lieutenant Claude A Bettington and Lieutenant Edward Hotchkiss, both of the Royal Flying Corps. Their aircraft was just five weeks old and of a new design coming into service. All flying of this aircraft, both in the UK and France was, as a result, suspended for two months. An inquest was held at the nearby Red Lion Inn in Wolvercote, its format setting a precedent for all future air crash investigations.

The two airmen killed were among the first military aviators to die in England. A memorial was placed on the Toll Bridge over the Thames (near the Trout Inn at Wolvercote) and over 2,000 people contributed towards its cost. The accident stunned Oxford at the time. The funeral procession through Oxford drew large crowds.

More details are found in Wright P (2015) The Royal Flying Corps in Oxfordshire. See reference no. 51.

Local accident – 2

An extract from an aviator's letter to his family states:

> Was at the 'drome today, when one of the best pilots looped three times and on his third loop pulled the bally machine apart. Wings came off. The engine was sunken about four feet in the ground. It caught fire, of course, and the pilot and the passenger didn't have a show.

> . . . Tonight in the mess everything was as usual. A stranger would never guess that the most popular member of our mess had been done for, just two hours previous, the same old chatter, the same kidding and joking, and nothing sad or morbid.

From Lieut. Patrick S Manley, a Canadian pilot under training at Port-meadow, in a letter dated the 15th March 1918, to Niagara University (six weeks before Rosemary Richardson joined the WRAF).

3. Manley shot down in France

Lieutenant Manley was taken prisoner after flying an 'aggressive patrol' over enemy lines in Northern France on the 27th September, and an emergency landing near Cambrai. He had secured five 'victories' over enemy aircraft over a nine-day period leading up to the 24th September 1918. Manley was flying a Bristol fighter with Lewis machine guns mounted on it. The British dropped a message behind enemy lines seeking news of his fate and whereabouts.

Manley survived the crash and was imprisoned by the Germans. He later returned to Ontario in Canada and died in 1952 in Ohio, USA.

Taken from www.communigate.co.uk/oxford/oxfordfreeman *and* www.theaerodrome.com/aces/canada/manley.php

Notes and references

Chapter 1: The early Richardson years

1. National Trust (1997) *Chastleton House: Oxfordshire*. Swindon: National Trust; National Trust (2013) *Chastleton House and Garden*, Swindon: National Trust.
2. National Trust and Ian Hilton (2011) *The Chastleton Diaries: Change and Continuity in the Nineteenth Century*. Swindon: National Trust.
3. Walter Jones was the most inventive member of the family. Apart from his work on croquet, he developed an automatic boot winder, and a type of alert system for use by ladies who felt themselves threatened in (non-corridor) railway carriages. One of his most forward-thinking ideas was to project advertisements onto the dome of St Pauls Cathedral after dark. Needless to say, this did not come to fruition! See 'Mission Improbable: The Croquet King', script for programme talk broadcast by the BBC on the 14th May 1994.
4. The Richardson family is listed in *The Cheshire Landed Gentry and Aristocracy, 1810*.
5. The six brothers and sisters, with estimated years of birth, were: Fanny (1850), Richard (1852), Helen (1855), Annie (1856), Louisa (1857) and Edward (1860).
6. The picture of Capenhurst Hall in 1888 is taken from John Marius Wilson's *Imperial Gazetteer of England and Wales: 1870–72*.
7. CTR's first marriage was to Lucy Bather in New Milverton, Warwickshire in 1888. Lucy died in 1889.

8. A Geoffrey Taswell Richardson was also born in Leamington, in 1897. He was the eldest son of the Reverend Edward Taswell Richardson, and subsequently joined the Royal Flying Corps.

9 See photos from *Country Life,* 19th July 1902.

10 Horn, P. (1986) *The Rise and Fall of the Victorian Servant.* Gloucester: Alan Sutton.

11 Oxfordshire Record Office, *File E24/1/F9/4*

12 In the 1861 census, Mrs Fanny Richardson (née Fanny Taswell) and the family are recorded at Grove House, on the Wirral. Mrs Fanny Richardson is listed as the wife of the incumbent at Capenhurst, Cheshire. Charles is seven years old at this point. There were seven servants at this address, including a footman, cook and two nursery maids. It is not known why the family were at Grove House on this particular census day.

13 www.norland.co.uk

14 Lethbridge, L. (2013) *Servants: A Downstairs View of Twentieth Century Britain*, Bloomsbury, London, pp39–40.

15 The Goldsmiths' Company, a craft guild, had been established in Chester around 1200.

16 Jones, R. (2009) *Chester and the Landscape Development of North East Wales (Part 4 – Post Medieval)* in Chester Society for Landscape History, Newsletter no. 45, Ashton Heyes, CH3 8DA, pp3–9; Ridgway, M. H. (1968) *Chester Goldsmiths: From Early Times to 1726*. Altrincham: Sherratt, p160ff.

17 This is the same Grosvenor Estate that owns large tracts of land and property in West London, including Regent Street.

18 Taken from notes by the Grosvenor Museum, Chester on their collection of silver.

19 Ridgway, Maurice H (1985) *Chester Silver 1727–1837*, Chichester: Phillimore and Co Ltd.

20 Richardson is reported as having interests in copper mining at Maentrog, in Caernarvonshire, where he put Farrington in charge of a mine at Drws-y-coed. See Rees, D. M. (1968)

'Copper Mining in North Wales' in *Archaelogica Cambrensis*, Vol CXVII, p175.

21 Reverend Richard Richardson (RR5) (1811–1885) left £22,950 in his will; this equates to £1.9 million at 2015 prices.

22 More detail on the clearing of land for tea estates is given by Weatherstone: 'This usually involved felling of the jungle, including any native tea plants, and then setting fire to it all . . . the tea plants were not the only ones who then burst forth with a vigorous growth, so too did the shoots from all the jungle tree stumps . . . all these required continual cutting back until they eventually died.' From Weatherstone, J. (1986) *The Pioneers 1825–1900: The Early British Tea and Coffee Planters and Their Way of Life*. London: Quiller, p40.

23 Gow, Wilson and Stanton (1897) *Tea Producing Companies of India and Ceylon*. London: GWS.

24 *St James Gazette*, 16th October 1895, p16.

25 Ibid., notes accompanying prospectus of 16th October.

26 *Local Government Gazette*, 3rd September 1891, p 9.

27 Roy, S (2011) *Historical Review of Tea Industries in India: A Study of Assam Tea*, 2011 International Conference on Social Sciences and Humanity, Singapore.

28 Personal communication from John Lampitt to Lawrie Thompson, Chastleton Research Group.

29 Bryans designed and installed a memorial window to Edith Cavell, the nurse who ran a training school for nurses in Brussels, and also helped over two hundred British and Allied soldiers to escape back to Britain. Cavell was executed by firing squad by the Germans in Belgium in 1917. The window is located at St Mary's Church in Swardesten near Norwich. See www.edithcavell.org.uk.

30 His glasswork is signed with a variously described 'greyhound', 'running dog', or 'running black hound' symbol. See Lampitt, J. and F. (2004) *Herbert Bryans and his Stained Glass*. Ely: Stained Glass Museum.

31 See BBC (2015) Isambard Kingdom Brunel (1806–59), www.bbc.uk/history. Also the Brunel archive at Bristol University contains a number of letters from Brunel to Richardson, all written in an immaculate copperplate style. There are also letters from Richardson to colleagues.

32 Griffin, P. (2010) 'Charles Richardson, Civil Engineer in Gloucestershire 1835–45' in *Gloucestershire Society for Industrial Archaeology Journal*, pp 28–38; Griffin, P. (2005) *The Journal of Charles Richardson, Civil Engineer, 1835–38: An Edited Transcription and Commentary*, MPhil Thesis, University of Gloucestershire.

33 www.espncricinfo/com.wisdenalmanack

34 The format for Wimbledon differed from that today. The men's singles competition resulted in an All-Comers Final. The winner of this then played the previous year's winner in a Challenge Round. Richardson was in the All-Comers Final. See www.tennisarchives.com

Chapter 2: The Great War 1914–1918

35 Information from Lawrie Thompson, Chastleton Research Group. *Moreton History*, Vol.14, No 1, 2009.

36 See www.redcross.org.uk/WW1 and the 'Gloucestershire Red Cross Hospitals 1914–19', at www.angelfire.com/az/garethknight/redcross/glosva

37 See 'Roll of Sons and Daughters of the Anglican Clergy throughout the World who gave their lives in the Great War 1914–1918' at www.archive.org/details/rollofsonsdaught00usshrich

38 Account of Major HF Bidder of the Royal Sussex Regiment, p 103 in Macdonald, L (1988) *1914–1918: Voices and Images of the Great War*. London: Penguin Books.

39 *War Diary* of Second Battalion of the Royal Warwickshire Regiment, consulted at Regimental Museum, Warwick. The best account of the Battle is given in Cherry, N. (2008) *Most*

Unfavourable Ground: The Battle of Loos. Solihull: Helion.

40 Cherry, N., Ibid.

41 Lewis, G. (2005) *Carson: The Man Who Divided Ireland.* London: Hambledon Continuum, pp 34–35.

42 National Archives, Service record of the Hon. Walter Seymour Carson, accessed February 2014.

43 Ibid.

44 Ibid.

45 Ibid.

46 Lewis, G. (2005) *Carson: The Man Who Divided Ireland.* London: Hambledon Continuum, p 35.

47 National Archives, WRAF application form for Rosemary Richardson, accessed February 2014.

48 Wright, P. (n.d.) 'The Women's Royal Air Force', *Cross and Cockade International,* The First World War Aviation Historical Society.

49 Ibid., pp 156–160.

50 See tape of interview with Colonel and Mrs Alexander (Rosemary Richardson) on 16/12/1992 in the National Trust sound archive.

51 Wright, P. (2015) *The Royal Flying Corps 1912–1918 in Oxford-shire,* 2nd edition. Peterborough: Cross and Cockade International.

52 Ibid.

53 Ibid.

54 A plaque relating to the Bettington crash is located in Wolver-cote Church (see Annex 1).

Chapter 3: The end of an era?

55 Until 1921 the ship sailed via the Cape, rather than Suez. See newspaper article 'Steamship to Sail via Suez to India', *New York Times,* January 16th, 1921.

56 Note from Chipping Norton History Society, Mr D. Nobbs.

57 Weatherstone, J (1986) *The Pioneers 1825–1900: The Early British Tea and Coffee Planters and Their Way of Life*. London: Quiller Press, pp63–65.

58 Copy of the Will of Charles Richardson, titled 'Death on or after 1ˢᵗ January 1898', from Lawrie Thompson.

59 This, and the next section, is taken from tapes of interviews with Colonel and Mrs Alexander, Dorothy Hadland and Betty Andrews, held by the National Trust.

60 This whole episode necessitated a trip to what Colonel Alexander termed 'the nether regions' (the servants' quarters), to find the whereabouts of his uniform. The fact that he referred to the nether regions in this way suggests he had not ventured there before, and that normally a strict demarcation was kept between the servants' quarters and the areas frequented by the family at this time.

61 Oxford Record Office; files no. E24/1/44 and E24/1/45.

62 National Trust (2013) Chastleton House and Garden, Swindon: National Trust.

63 Ibid.

64 Lethbridge, L. (2013) *Servants: A Downstairs View of Twentieth Century Britain*, Bloomsbury, London, pp39–40.

65 See tapes of interview with Colonel and Mrs Alexander (Rosemary Richardson) in 1992, National Trust.

66 The fullest account of the regiment is given in Watson, Major General W. A. (2005) *King George's Own Central India Horse: The Story of a Local Corps*. Uckfield, East Sussex: Naval and Military Press, (A reprint from the original printed in 1929). 2nd Lieut A A S Alexander (sic) is listed in this volume as posted to the regiment during the Great War, see p 460.

67 The successful Palestine campaign is comprehensively covered in Bruce, A. (2013) *The Last Crusade: The Palestine Campaign in the First World War*. London: John Murray, especially pp 288–342.

68 Taken from Augustus Alexander's records in the Liddle Collection in Leeds University Library; GB 206; tape 330.

69 Gordon, C. (2009) *Cotswold Arts and Crafts Architecture*. Chichester: Phillimore.

70 Japanning is the art of coating surfaces of metal, wood and papier mâché with japan or varnish, which is dried and hardened by means of a high temperature in stoves and hot chambers. The process appears to have been introduced to Birmingham by John Taylor. When he died in 1775, Taylor was worth £300,000 and the value of his weekly production was £2,000. One of Taylor's rivals was John Baskerville who, using profits from his successful japanning business, set up his own printing presses in 1750, designing typefaces to print books and pamphlets. The meetings between Taylor and Samuel Johnson are referred to in Volume 1 of *The Letters of Samuel Johnson*.

71 An article on the Taylor family can be found on the *Birmingham Grid for Learning* at <u>www.bgfl.org</u>